*Questions and Answers
on Death and Dying*

BY ELISABETH KÜBLER-ROSS

On Death and Dying
To Live Until We Say Good-Bye
Living with Death and Dying
Remember the Secret
Death: The Final Stage of Growth
On Children and Death
Working It Through
AIDS: The Ultimate Challenge

Questions and Answers on Death and Dying

Elisabeth Kübler-Ross, M.D.

Collier Books
Macmillan Publishing Company
New York

Maxwell Macmillan Canada
Toronto

Maxwell Macmillan International
New York Oxford Singapore Sydney

Collier Books	Maxwell Macmillan Canada, Inc.
Macmillan Publishing Company	1200 Eglinton Avenue East
866 Third Avenue	Suite 200
New York, NY 10022	Don Mills, Ontario M3C 3N1

Macmillan Publishing Company is part of the Maxwell Communication
Group of Companies.

Library of Congress Cataloging-in-Publication Data
Kübler-Ross, Elisabeth.
Questions and answers on death and dying / Elisabeth Kübler-Ross.
—1st Collier Books trade ed.
p. cm.
Previously published: Macmillan, 1974.
Includes index.
ISBN 0-02-089142-3
1. Death. 2. Terminal care. I. Title.
R726.8.K8   1993   93-9167   CIP
616.07 ' 8—dc20

Macmillan books are available at special discounts for bulk purchases
for sales promotions, premiums, fund-raising, or educational use. For
details, contact: Special Sales Director, Macmillan Publishing Company,
866 Third Avenue, New York, NY 10022.

First Collier Books Edition 1974

First Collier Books Trade Edition 1993

10 9 8 7 6 5 4 3 2

Printed in the United States of America

Contents

Introduction

Since the publication of my first book, *On Death and Dying* (Macmillan, 1969), an increasing number of health professionals, lay people, and institutions have become involved with the needs of the terminally ill patient and his family.

Over the past five years I have participated in approximately seven-hundred workshops, lectures, and seminars on the care of dying patients. The participants came from every conceivable area of health care. There were physicians, members of the clergy, nurses, social workers, inhalation and occupational therapists, rehabilitation workers, ambulance drivers, funeral directors, as well as lay people who often had experienced the loss of a loved one. They came to seek answers to the many questions they brought with them.

This book is an attempt to answer some of the questions most frequently posed to me by audiences. Where they have been edited, it is only for clarification.

A book of this size can never answer all the questions. The most frequently asked questions regard the dying patient, and the largest portion of this book deals with patient-related issues. The next most frequently asked questions deal with staff problems and interdisciplinary teamwork. Special issues are covered in shorter chapters to make for easier reading.

I have specifically excluded chapters on "Religion and Life after Death" as well as chapters on "Bereavment and Grief." This was done not only because of lack of space, but because there are others who are more qualified to answer these questions.

Again, as in my book, *On Death and Dying,* I have focused almost exclusively on the adult patient. Questions and answers relating to children will be published in my forthcoming book, *On Children and Death* (Macmillan).

With the increasing number of inservice education programs for hospital personnel, seminars for medical students and other health professionals, and pastoral training centers, this book may stimulate discussion in areas where we have too often avoided the issue—not because we do not care, but because we feel so helpless in the face of the many unanswered questions arising at the time of this final crisis.

*Questions and Answers
on Death and Dying*

1

The Dying Patient

The dying patient has to pass through many stages in his struggle to come to grips with his illness and his ultimate death. He may deny the bad news for a while and continue to work "as if he were as well and strong as before." He may desperately visit one physician after the other in the hope that the diagnosis was not correct. He may wish to shield his family (or his family may want to shield him) from the truth.

Sooner or later he will have to face the grim reality, and he often reacts with an angry "why me" to his illness. If we learn to assist this angry patient rather than to judge him—if we learn not to take his anguish as a personal insult—he will then be able to pass to the third stage, the stage of bargaining. He may bargain with God for an extension of life, or he may promise good behavior and religious dedication if he is spared more suffering. He will try to "put his house in order" and "finish unfinished business" before he really admits, "This is happening to me."

In the depression stage he mourns past losses first and then begins to lose interest in the outside world.

He reduces his interests in people and affairs, wishes to see fewer and fewer people and silently passes through preparatory grief. If he is allowed to grieve, if his life is not artificially prolonged and if his family has learned "to let go," he will be able to die with peace and in a stage of acceptance. (Examples of these stages are described in detail in my book, *On Death and Dying*, (Macmillan, 1969).

The following questions come from patients and relatives, physicians and nurses, and hopefully allow the reader to identify with the patient and to feel more comfortable when he or she is faced with a similar problem.

TELLING THE PATIENT

When is the time for an attending physician to tell his terminally ill patient of his diagnosis?

As soon as the diagnosis is confirmed a patient should be informed that he is seriously ill. He should then be given hope immediately, and by this I mean he should be told of all the treatment possibilities. We usually then wait until the patient asks for more details. If he asks for specifics I would give him an honest, straightforward answer. I do not tell the patient that he is dying or that he is terminally ill. I simply tell him that he is seriously ill and that we are trying to do everything humanly possible to help him to function as well as he can.

Whose responsibility is it to inform the patient of his terminal illness? The doctor or the minister?

The doctor has the priority, but he may delegate this job to the minister.

Should every patient be told that he is dying?

No patient should be told that he is dying. I do not encourage people to force patients to face their own death when they are not ready for it. Patients should be told that they are seriously ill. When they are ready to bring up the issue of death and dying, we should answer them, we should listen to them, and we should hear the questions, but you do not go around telling patients they are dying and depriving them of a glimpse of hope that they may need in order to live until they die.

What can be done when the doctor refuses to tell the patient about his terminal illness? Do you suggest that someone else tell the patient? If so, who? Can he or she do it even without the doctor's permission?

No, you cannot do it without the doctor's permission. Unless the physician gives a minister or a nurse, or social worker the explicit request to do his job for him, it is inappropriate to do so unless you are the patient's next-of-kin.

When does the patient begin to die and when, then, does our relationship begin to be one with a dying patient?

In our interdisciplinary workshops on death and dying our relationships started with the hospitalization of the patients who had a potentially terminal illness. I believe, however, that such preparation should start much earlier and that we should teach our children and our young people to face the reality of death. They would then not have to go through all the stages when

they are terminally ill and have so little time to deal
with unfinished business. You live a different quality
of life, as you do when you have faced your finiteness.

*One situation which leaves me uncomfortable is when
I know a patient has a terminal illness and the family
of the patient has not been told. I think it is only fair
to know if one is dying. Must we rely on the physician
to tell them?*

A patient has the right to be told how seriously ill
he is and I believe that the family also has to be
notified of the seriousness of an illness. It is the physician who has to relay this news to them. If the physician is unable to do so, the patient or the family should
then approach other members of a helping profession
and ask them. This is usually the chaplain, the priest,
the rabbi, or the nurse. If another member of the
helping profession is asked directly by the family or the
patient, it is his duty to inform the physician of these
needs, and, if necessary, ask that the job be delegated.

DIFFICULTIES IN COMMUNICATION

*Do you suggest that doctors talk to a patient's family
outside the sick room rather than when standing beside
the bed of a comatose patient?*

I try to teach my medical students, externs and
interns, early that comatose patients are often able to
hear and are quite aware of what is going on in the
room. Since I am very much in favor of being open
and honest with critically ill patients, I find no difficulty in the patient's hearing me share with the family

the seriousness of the illness. If I have to share something with a family that I do not want the patient to hear, then I would naturally go outside the patient's room, preferably to a private office.

How do you cope with a family who refuses to allow any mention of "it" to their dying relatives?

I try to sit alone with the patient and then he will relate to me what he has not been able to relate to his own family. We then have to spend extra time sitting with the family separately and attempting to help them to deal with the situation which the patient has already faced.

I took care of a terminal cancer patient about two years ago who asked questions like, "How sick am I?"; "Am I going to get well?"; "What's wrong with me?"; "Why doesn't anyone tell me anything?" When I approached the attending physician regarding his patient's needs, he became very upset and asked me, "What do you want me to do, tell her she's going to die?" He had tears in his eyes when he said this. Would you care to comment on this kind of situation?

Yes, I think this is a very caring physician who obviously is involved and who obviously is bothered that this patient is not going to get well. I would express my empathy to him. I would tell him that it must be very hard to take care of patients like this. Then I would very gingerly ask him if it is all right if I talk with her. He may then give you permission to talk with her because he is apparently too upset to do it himself.

You've talked about talking about death, but what do you say, for example, if someone wants to know why he is dying? What do you say?

I tell him that I don't know, and ask him, "What are you really asking me?" The patient will then proceed to say he has worked all his life long, that he was just ready for retirement and why is it happening now. Or he will say, "My children are too young; they have not even started high school yet. If God would give me only a few more years to live to see my children grow up." If you sit there and listen, the patient will do most of the talking. All this will help him to express his feelings. You cannot go into a patient's room with a prepared statement of what you are going to say. You say what feels right at the moment and when you don't know what to say, you simply admit that fact, too.

How do you work with a patient who tells you about terrible pains and shows you the lumps?

I try to give him adequate pain relief first so he doesn't have to complain of terrible pains. If he shows me the lumps it means he wants to demonstrate how sick he is or how much he's suffering. He's obviously asking for empathy, which I try to give him.

In talking to a dying person with whom you've been close, are you supposed to be honest about your feelings of fear, loss, separation, i.e., stop playing games?

Yes.

What is the best stage to approach a patient about death?

You do not approach a patient about death. You wait until he brings up the topic of death and dying. If he talks about his pain, you talk about his pain. If he expresses a fear of death, you sit down and listen to him and ask what he is specifically afraid of. If he wants to make funeral arrangements or a last will long before he is close to dying, you don't try to talk him out of it but help him get a lawyer and put his house in order.

I am concerned about physicians who cannot answer questions in a straightforward way. When a patient asks if he has cancer and the doctor does not say no, there is only one option: "I do not know yet." A refusal to say one or the other will be interpreted by the patient as a tacit yes, and with no indication of how serious his condition is he may suspect he is in pretty terrible shape and this may hasten his demise.

I don't think it will hasten the patient's demise. It may give him some sleepless nights, it may make him worry and wonder, it may give him more anxieties, perhaps, but sooner or later he will again ask the physician a straightforward question. If he still does not receive an answer, he will try to find out through his family, his minister, nurse, or social worker about the true state of his health. Hopefully, one of his friends or a member of the hospital staff will then answer his questions.

My husband has emphysema and has been unable to work for the past four years. He is getting weaker but is still not quite house-bound. We both have our hang-ups; we are in our sixties and we have never talked about death and dying. Should we bring this topic up?

I think if you are already coming to a workshop on death and dying that implies to me that you are curious about it. You would like to help your husband and you have at least some questions about it. Why don't you go home and tell your husband about this workshop. If he changes the topic of conversation you will know that he is uncomfortable and doesn't want to talk about it. If he asks you any questions, you will be in the midst of a discussion on death and dying. You may then ask him if there is anything—such as the matter of a last will or other things—that might be easier to take care of now.

How do you deal with a fourteen-year-old who keeps saying she is going to die when she is eighteen years old? She is seriously ill.

I would listen to her and believe that she may know more than we do.

I have a client who is terminally ill. His wife had a heart attack recently and cannot be told the true nature of his problem yet. What is the best way of relating this to her?

I think a wife who has had a heart attack recently, and who knows that her husband is ill and unable to visit, will have more anxieties, more concerns, and will be more upset if nobody communicates with her about the nature of her husband's problems. I would sit with the wife, tell her that I just came from visiting the husband, and function as a messenger between the husband and wife, both of whom are hospitalized. I do not know if this couple is hospitalized in the same hospital; if they are they should preferably be together once the wife is out of the coronary care unit and in somewhat better condition. If not, they should be allowed to visit each other so that they can talk and at least share what they feel can be shared without unduly upsetting each other.

Can you say more about deciding where to put your help when the family and patient are present and the need of the family is greater?

You always help the ones who need the help the most.

How should you approach a person of whom you have no knowledge except the fact that he is dying?

You walk into the room, ask if he feels like talking for a few minutes and then you sit down and ask what it is that he needs most, and "Is there anything that I can do for you?" Sometimes they ask you to simply sit down and hold their hand; sometimes they wave you away because they want to be alone. Or you ask if there is anybody else you can get for them. That is very often what a patient needs—a specific person whom he chooses. You then get that person and you have helped that patient. Sometimes when I feel like talking and I don't know the patient at all, I say, "Is it tough?" or "Do you feel like talking about it?" and in no time he talks about what really bothers him.

How do you help parents accept the oncoming death of a nineteen-year-old son and speak about it with the son? Both realize death is coming, but don't verbalize together. Father and mother don't feel they can talk about it with the son.

Sometimes they need a catalyst, and this can be you. You can say to the parents, "Wouldn't it help if you expressed some of your concerns and feelings with your son? It may make it easier for him to complete some unfinished business between the three of you." If they are unable to do so, don't push, but at least share with them some of your clinical experiences. When this has been done, this may encourage them to open up.

How do you give a patient a clue that you will talk about death with him or her if he wants it?

I sit with him and talk about his illness, his pain, his hopes, and in a short time we are very often talking about our philosophies of life and death. Without any big preparations, we are in the midst of some real issues. Sometimes you can sit with a patient and ask him if he is willing to share with you what it is like to be so very ill. The patient will then talk about all the turmoil he has gone through and will perhaps add, "Sometimes I wonder if I would be better off to die." This gives you the opening to talk about what feelings, ideas, fears, and fantasies he has about death and dying.

I am a member of a helping profession, and very often upon entering the room of the patient have very nega-tive gut reactions. How do you suggest that I make contact with such patients? You said, "I share my feelings." I like that, but does that apply here when you have negative feelings?

Sometimes a patient makes you very angry and you feel like taking off. I feel quite comfortable telling a patient that sometimes his behavior irritates me, makes me angry, and maybe if we try to talk about it, we can find ways and solutions so that he does not alienate all the staff. If I'm open and frank about my reactions to him, the patient not only has a way of expressing his anger, but he knows I'm honest with him and he will be more frank and comfortable with me.

When learning how to communicate with patients about death and dying, is it always safe to verbalize your gut feelings to the patient? I say "safe" because I haven't identified my own feelings on death and dying and relating with other people and, therefore, I'm not sure how helpful my feelings would be to the patient.

It is not always safe to verbalize your own feelings. If you come into a patient's room and your gut reaction is, "I hope she doesn't die on me," you naturally don't share this with a patient. If your gut reaction is one of insecurity and helplessness and yet you would truly like to help this patient, it would be "very safe" to tell the patient, "I am not sure how I can help you though I would like to. Is there anything specific I can do for you that would make you more comfortable?" I quite often tell my patients that I feel somewhat helpless or at a loss for words and sit down waiting for a cue from the patient to help me out. These patients then become very comfortable with me because they are able to share their own feelings of ambivalence, of insecurity, and, sometimes, of helplessness with me. Together we try to find solutions.

To what extent is it possible or desirable to talk with a cardiac patient about the seriousness of his heart attack? One does not want to frighten the patient so much that he has another attack which then brings on death.

This fear of talking with cardiac patients about the seriousness of their coronaries is our problem and not realistic. A patient is very aware when he has had a serious heart attack. He should be informed about the seriousness in order to take his diet, his exercise, and his posthospital care seriously. A patient is much more frightened, much more anxious, and much more prone to difficulties if you are not honest with him. He may continue to eat excessively or be so intimidated by the whole experience that he does not dare to exercise at all, which may result in another coronary. We talk openly and frankly with our cardiac patients. We tell them how serious the attack was and at the same time we give them information as to their limits of functioning, encouraging them to follow through with their exercises in order to have a better prognosis.

Since you do not believe in telling a patient a concrete number of months or years of life expectancy, would you agree that it is good to tell him the chances of survival at specific periods of time such as three months, or one year, or two years, or five years?

We have found that patients who have been given a specific number of months of life expectancy, do not do well. Our prognosis is not that accurate that we can tell a patient how much time he has to live. If we tell a man that he has six months to live and he survives the six months, he is often in a very difficult predicament in that he is no longer living and not able to die. I think it is much more honest to say that we do not know, the chances look very slim at this time. If he insists on specifics, the physician should then give him some statistical approximations so that he has some idea of how long he has to put his house in order.

How do you assist patients in not feeling guilty for sharing their feelings in relation to their own death? For example, I have had many patients who, after crying, find it difficult to continue with an open relationship even though I try to continue supporting them.

I do not think they stop having a relationship with you because they shared their grief and their own feelings. They have probably been able to work through their anger and their reactive depression and are now in the process of a preparatory grief during which time they are beginning to "wean off," that is to separate and to decathect.* This means that they will look for fewer interpersonal relationships. They want to see acquaintances and relatives once more, then the children once more, and at the end they usually like to maintain a relationship with one or two people, usually their immediate next-of-kin.

How would you approach the subject of death when dealing with people who are continually faced with possibility of death but are never "condemned," as with a coronary patient?

* The opposite of cathesis, which is attachment, conscious or unconscious of emotional feeling and significance to an idea or object, most commonly a person (American Psychiatric Association, *A Psychiatric Glossary* [Washington, D.C., 1969]).

There are many patients who are continuously faced with the possibility of death. These patients have to come to grips with their own finiteness. Then they are able to live a very different quality of life, knowing that death can occur anytime, but hoping that there will still be many more weeks and months ahead. These patients should not be avoided; they are the ones who should face the reality of their own death as early as possible.

How does a professional person respond to a nonprofessional person when told that "You are cold and indifferent to death"?

I would look into the mirror and question whether there is not some truth in the statement. If I do not feel cold and indifferent toward this person's death and the grief of the family, I would regard it as part of the anger that this family is now going through in relation to the recent loss.

When a family is in a stage of anger, especially after a sudden, unexpected loss, they often displace their anger onto nondeserving members of the health team. If it is unjustified, simply accept it as an expression of their turmoil.

What dangers, if any, are there in becoming too involved emotionally with feelings of terminal patients?

If you have a good team approach where other members of your staff watch over you and with whom you can share your own feelings, there is very little danger in becoming too involved. If you are working full time and in solo practice with many dying patients, there is a risk that you will get too involved, and thus too drained emotionally and physically. No one should work exclusively with dying patients. It is not possible to do this on a full-time basis.

Does one develop through experience an intuition that says, "Yes, now he is talking about his death"? Do you sometimes misfire? Does the patient sometimes "announce" his own death prematurely, or is his intuition always accurate?

I do not know if this is intuition that says, "Yes, now he is talking about his death." I think if you can hear and listen to patients, you'll know when they are talking about their own impending death and will respond to it. Naturally, all of us misfire once in a while. The patient occasionally is concerned about his own premature death when, in fact, he has a fairly good prognosis. It is important to make the differential diagnosis between a pathological fear of death, where the concern of one's death arises with every little symptom, and a "message" from the patient who is terminally ill and who senses that his days are counted. Rather than intuition, I would say that experience and the art of listening will help you to misfire less often.

Should one try to get the patient and the patient's family on the same level, that is to say, at the same "stage" of dying? For example, anger, denial, acceptance?

That is a utopic dream and I don't think this works. This is, again, projecting our own needs rather than accepting people wherever they are and being available when and if they are ready to move on to the next stage.

How do you handle the Lazareth syndrome?—i.e., the dying patient prepared for death who goes on to recover?

I would rejoice with him.

DENIAL AS A FIRST LINE OF DEFENSE

How would you work with a patient who shows clinical evidence of cancer, but who refuses further diagnostic studies such as bronchoscopy or an exploratory operation for apparent cancer of the lung, or X rays to determine if the cancer is operable and/or likely to benefit from radiation treatment?

A patient has the right to refuse treatment. I think you should level with him, you should tell him what you suspect, and you should give him the option, but it is up to him to reject it or to accept your offer.

Why is it that many doctors still refuse to tell patients that they have terminal illnesses? Is this trend changing?

There are many physicians who are uncomfortable about telling their patients they are seriously ill, but the trend is changing. More and more physicians are beginning to be comfortable about this. We now have more medical schools who include the care of the dying patient in their curriculum. With medical students having had some instruction, some lectures or workshops, and some assistance during their formative years, there is a good chance that there will be more physicians in the near future who will be comfortable with dying patients.

What does a nursing staff do with the patient who has gone through the whole dying process and remains in the stage of denial?

They naturally allow the patient to stay in the stage of denial and treat him like any other patient.

Please tie in the stages of dying with loss of sight. I'm now working with a woman who is losing her sight and is in the denial stage. The doctor has not told her yet. What is my role as a social worker?

Listen to her. This patient will share with you her horrible fear of becoming blind. You then let her talk about it. Tell her about talking books, about the white cane, about the seeing eye dog, about all the people who can live a very normal life in spite of being blind. Don't tell her it's not terrible, but simply tell her that blind people can function like sighted ones. She will then be comfortable and able to talk with you about it if her doctor is too uncomfortable to do so. All my patients that became blind have gone through the same stages as my dying patients. I have worked with blind patients for fifteen years and I'm very impressed with the fact that they are going through the same stages as anyone else who is in the process of losing something very important.

Must we wait until a patient has been told before we try to help him? How can we reach out to the patient who does not seem to progress from the stage of denial?

We must not wait until the patient has been told about his illness before we help him. There are many

ways we can help him. We have to understand the
symbolic language that patients use when they remain
in the stage of denial and yet talk about their dying.
We can give them comfort: physical, spiritual, and
emotional. We can sit down with them and say, "It's
tough, isn't it?" and these remarks will very often open
up the floodgates and the patient will talk with you
about his fear, his discomfort, or his fantasies.

*A patient with a history of cancer (surgery two years
previously) is advised readmission for symptoms, but
instead goes to Florida for the winter. Is this denial?
His wife goes along with his decision and goes on this
journey.*

A patient who has had cancer two years before and
has a readmission for similar symptoms probably
senses that this is now a recurrence of his cancer. He
also probably knows that the months, perhaps the years
ahead, will be filled with hospitalizations and less and
less functioning. It may be his way of saying, "Let's live
it up once more. Let's get this trip to Florida in so that
we can at least have a memory of having been together in Florida, a dream that we were always dream-
ing about but were never able to fulfill." After he has
completed this unfinished business he will most likely
return to the hospital and be a much better patient
than if he always nostalgically thinks, "If I had only
gone to Florida with my wife." It is, again, important
that we do not judge these patients because they do not
gratify our needs for an immediate hospitalization and
that we do not necessarily label them as "denial." All
that it means is that this man has made a choice; it is
his choice and his right to make it.

What does a nursing staff do with patients who stay in a complete denial until their death?

They treat them just like any other needy human being and remember that some people need denial and that this should not be broken artificially just because we would like them to drop their denial.

A man has an inoperable cancer, but the doctors say he probably will be able to live almost normally for a year or so before the decline begins. The wife has decided not to tell him as long as he is living in reasonably good health, then tell him. He should still have enough time to "get his affairs in order." Is this the right approach?

This may be the right approach for some patients who need denial themselves, to tell them as late as possible, but this is the exception to the rule. Most patients do better if they are told early that they are seriously ill, but are allowed to have hope, *i.e.*, that he can live normally for a reasonable length of time. If the patient should ask the physician directly whether he has a malignancy or not, the patient has the right to be told, and if he is not informed, the physician may in certain circumstances be liable to a suit later on.

Mr. X, age twenty-two, with cancer, claims to have been miraculously healed. However, all indications are that he is in terminal stages. What role can we play? Is he simply playing this game for the family's sake and does he really recognize his true state?

If a young man with terminal cancer makes a statement that he is miraculously healed, this means to me that he wants to believe in a miracle in spite of the fact that from a medical point of view he's regarded as terminally ill. I would sit with him and say, "Yes, miracles do sometimes happen" and wait for a while and continue to visit with him so that he has an opportunity to share with you his feelings about his terminal illness or his belief that he has been cured. It is not your role, whether you are a member of a helping profession or a family member, to break down a defense. It is your role to help the patient, and if he needs to believe that he is cured, it is cruel and untherapeutic to tell him there are no such things as miracles. If you do not believe, yourself, that miracles do happen sometimes, you can simply ask him to tell you more about it. He may even end up convincing you. Over the last eight years we have had several patients who had been given up, and from a medical point of view had no practical chance of recovery, but who are still alive several years after the predicted date of their death.

I have a patient dying now. She's behaving as if she doesn't know it or she may be denying it. How can I grind this out? How can I make her comfortable and what can I talk about?

I think it is important that you do not "grind it out." If she appears to be in pain ask her if she has enough pain relief. If she is restless, sit with her and hold her hand and ask her simply, "What can I do to make you comfortable?" The patient will then tell you what her needs are. I think we are always trying to play a strange guessing game, perhaps pretending to ourselves that we are all-knowing, omnipotent human beings. If you don't know how to help a patient, simply ask her. She may tell you to get a special friend in or she may tell you to get a member of the clergy. She may want to put her house in order or to make a last will. These requests tell you that she knows that she is dying.

You said at one time that every dying person should have one human being who does not need to deny death. Is there such a person or don't we all have our own style of denial?

There are many people who do not deny the reality of death. It requires a long working-through process in our death denying society, but once you have faced your own finiteness and have accepted it, you will see that life becomes much more meaningful and more valuable. Those people who have truly faced their own finiteness will be much better equipped to help dying patients.

WHY ME?

Can you give a few more suggestions of how to handle a patient when he asks, "Why me?"

I tell them, "I don't know why you," but you may ask the question the other way around, "Why not you?" Since all of us have to face death and dying it has to happen to any one of us sooner or later. He is really asking "Why is it happening to me now?" I would let him raise this question so that he will then be able to express his anger and anguish and ventilate all his feelings of dismay and other concerns. This will give you cues as to how to help him.

I am a terminally ill patient. When I first found out about my condition I realized that my future had been taken away from me. I was very angry. Have you seen similar feelings?

Most of my patients react the same way. They are shocked and they are angry that their future has been taken away, but gradually they realize that they are still living today, that they still have a tomorrow. Because they have a limited time to live, very often they live with more intensity, with different values, and enjoy life more because they do not always plan for tomorrow and next year, the way healthy people do.

A patient is crying and states that his physician just told him that he is going to die. A medical student wonders how to respond to such a patient.

If you are comfortable enough to say so, I would say to him that nobody knows when we are going to die, that he is critically ill, but that we are going to try to do everything in our power to see if we can give him another chance. If a patient is told that he is going to die without being given a glimpse of hope, this is very cruel and very often the patient gives up and spends his last days or weeks suffering.

What does the helping person (nurse, doctor, social worker) do with his own very strong reactions of tears or anger when he fears he cannot control himself? Sometimes this is the most important reason for avoiding the dying patient.

Every helping person needs a screaming room— perhaps a little room beside the nursing station, the hospital chapel, or any other room where you can cry, where you can curse, where you can express your anger, where you can disappear with a friend and tell nasty things about your co-workers who aggravated you or prevented you from staying with a needy patient. If we had some facilities like screaming rooms, the staff could ventilate their own feelings and would then be much more able to keep in a certain framework of control when they are back on the ward. This is especially true of people who work in intensive care units where it is very difficult to work for eight or nine hours without letting your feelings go occasionally.

How do you deal with rage and anger? If you meet it with acceptance this can be cruel, but to meet it with anger can also be cruel. How?

A patient who is angry and nasty and displaces all his discontentment and envy onto his friends and relatives and the staff can be very difficult for the people who take care of him. If you are faced with such a patient, you try to discover whether he has a reasonable justification for his anger. If, for example, the food is miserable, then you talk to the dietician to improve the food. If what he is going through is the true stage of anger in the process of dying where he asks, "why me?" then you try to tell him that you can appreciate his anger and his envy and that if you were in his position you would be angry, too. In other words, you try to put fuel in the fire and let him ventilate his anguish without making him feel guilty, without giving him the feeling that you are "above him" or belittling him. A few extra minutes spent with these extra-difficult patients can work wonders. They will call for the nurses less often, the family is more content, and the patients are more comfortable.

*How do you help resolve the panic and sense of not
enough time of a young couple where one has a slowly
progressive chronic neurological illness and they both
feel there is not enough time in the day or year left to
do all that they want to do with their lives together?*

The sense of panic and not enough time is a tempo-
rary anxiety. They will soon discover that being together cannot be counted in hours, weeks, or months,
but in the depth of their encounter. They may hear of
other couples who lose a partner in a sudden death
and they will learn to appreciate the blessing of having
had some extra time together and using it to its fullest.

*How do you help a person who is angry toward God?
We are so shocked and this is seen almost as a personal
attack.*

I would help him to express his anger toward God
because God is certainly great enough to be able to
accept it.

Why do some patients use profanity?

Patients who are terminally ill are not any different
from healthy people. Profanity can be used as a strong
weapon to deal with your own impotent rage.

*How do you "help" the family when they have become
abusive of the nursing staff? You know their anger
and anxieties, but they don't.*

The fact that you write the word "help" in quotes
already reflects that you have some ambivalent feelings toward them. I wonder if you really want to help
them or if you'd rather keep them quiet. If you can

learn not to take this abuse and insult personally, but see them as a troubled, anguished family in a great turmoil, then you may be able to help them ventilate their anguish and anger and they will become much more bearable to the nursing staff. Ideally, the family should be able to turn to somebody outside of the nursing staff, preferably a minister or social worker, who can help not only the family, but indirectly also the nursing staff who goes through this difficult period.

You said to one of your patients looking at his get-well cards on the wall, "Aren't you angry?" It worked out obviously, but weren't you projecting your own anger and not making a statement about where the patient was?

Yes, I shared with him my own gut reactions of rage and anger at the wall covered with phony get-well-soon cards when everybody who sent him a card obviously knew he was in the final stages of his life and totally unlikely ever to recover. Because I was able to share my own reactions, "I hit the nail on the head," enabling him to share his own rage and anger with me, obviously feeling better afterward.

BARGAINING—DEPRESSION AND GRIEF USUALLY FOLLOW

When a patient has been in one stage of dying and returns to an earlier stage does this mean that the earlier stage was not resolved?

No. I hope that I am making it clear that patients do not necessarily follow a classical pattern from the stage of denial to the stage of anger, to bargaining, to depression and acceptance. Most of my patients have exhibited two or three stages simultaneously and these do not always occur in the same order. It is, however, important to recognize that when a patient has reached a genuine, true stage of acceptance and he begins to regress, this is often because we do not allow the patient to let go. We may add unnecessary life-prolonging procedures which the patient does not appreciate anymore, or he may have a family member who hangs on and makes him guilty for dying on them. It is in this last stage especially that a regression is usually a sign of our inappropriate handling of the patient. This is not true in the other stages.

My sister has cancer and she is at the stage of bargaining at this time. She speaks freely of the cancer and the treatment. She laughs about dying "when the time comes" and has a big desire for one more trip in two years. Can a dying person go through one or more stages without it showing to those near and dear to them?

Your sister seems to be able to talk about it comfortably and to express a wish that she is still able to make another trip in two years. She seems to be in good spirits and I think you should be grateful that she is able to talk about it openly. People can go through a stage of bargaining without an outsider seeing it, but I would regard it as difficult to hide a genuine stage of anger or depression.

What do you say to a patient who is sick but not terminally ill and says, "I want to die tonight"?

I would say to him that I have felt this way sometimes, but I wonder what makes him think about it.

This will convey to him that all of us think about this occasionally. I'm more curious about what stimulated this statement.

Sometimes patients have a premonition of impending death and will share this with you if you listen to them. Don't stop them with statements like "oh, don't talk like that!"

A difficult pastoral situation I have presently is how to help a patient who has had a catastrophic threatening serious illness which we all considered fatal and who succeeded in coming to a degree of acceptance of the imminence of death, but then discovered that instead of dying his sentence is to face severe invalidism.

Sometimes facing death is easier than facing a long life with a serious handicap. If you have been successful in your pastoral counseling helping this patient to accept the imminence of his death, it is most likely that with some additional help, you will also be able to help him face a longer life with limited functioning. All of our patients who have multiple sclerosis, or are paraplegic, or are blind had to go through these stages. It is sometimes more difficult and requires more time to accept this limited life functioning than to face death, which is at least an end to the suffering.

How do you deal with the person who does not want to live?

It is too general a question. There are people who certainly do not want to live and I can empathize with them. There are patients who are totally paralyzed from head to toe who are aphasic, which means that they cannot say one single word, who cannot read and write anymore, who just lie in bed for years staring at you, fully conscious, tube-fed, and not able to communicate with the outer world except through their looks. The way they look at you they may be able to smile, they may be able to cry, and that is the only way they can have any contact with the outer world. Would you like to live this way?

I have cancer patients who have lived for months and months with tremendous pain, unable to move because of their bone metastasis, dependent upon relatives to turn them around, to feed them, to take care of their needs. If they go to a hospital they have the additional burden of horrendous expenses, which the family is barely able to pay. They know the outcome and they, too, do not want to live any longer. Would you like to live this way? I think we have to evaluate each patient. If the patient, under very understandable circumstances, expresses the wish to die soon, I have no problems sharing this hope with him.

A man was given only one day to live over two weeks ago. His physician had given up and done all he could, he said. Today the man survives and is apparently doing better. The family expected his death, but doesn't have much courage to face it. They are living on hope. The man does not want to see his wife. He claims everybody upsets him.

I think I would be upset too if somebody told me that I had only one day to live. None of our patients would do well if they had been given a specific number of days or weeks for their survival. This is an irresponsible way of communicating with patients because we never know whether or not the patient is an exception to the rule. Many of them have lived far beyond our medical expectations. This man is probably in between; he's not able to live and enjoy himself and he's not able to die; he's angry and everybody around him upsets him because they are kind of standing around waiting for his death to occur and death does not occur. I think somebody who feels comfortable talking with patients like this should go in and visit him, level with him, and say this was a silly statement that he had only one day to live. They should then sit together and discuss how he can be helped now that he has recuperated to some degree. He should be encouraged to use to the fullest whatever time he has. The patient will probably first ventilate some rage and anger followed by some statements as to what he wants to do with the time he has left.

What can we say about the psychiatric patients who feel almost dead, technically dead, without almost any hope for a future, much less a reasonably healthy future?

There are many partial deaths. Many patients in state hospitals, many elderly people in nursing homes are vegetating and merely existing but not truly living. This is what I regard as a partial death, especially if the future looks grim, if they have no caring family, if they have no chance of ever leading a normal, functioning life. It is up to us, the healthy people, to give these patients a chance so that they can start to live again and not have to look forward to death to release them from their chronic and long and hopeless suffering. Every human being has something to give if we would only allow its expression.

Patients with spinal cord paralysis, hemiplegia, amputations, often describe themselves as "half dead" or desiring to die. Do your concepts apply to them and if so, how? What can we do to assist them, especially when it often cannot be determined whether the paralysis will be permanent?

The many patients who have to face a paralysis have to come to grips with this tremendous loss. We have seen many Vietnam veterans paralyzed and many of them asked why they were not allowed to die. Many of these young men regard themselves as "half dead." This is a very understandable reaction and it takes time, patience, love, and endurance to counsel with them and to help them find some meaning in their suffering, and, most important of all, to show them that even a paralyzed person can live a meaningful life. These patients will very typically go through the stage of shock and denial; they will not believe that they are permanently paralyzed. When it begins to dawn on them that there may be no recuperation they will become very angry and difficult patients. They may bargain with God; they may become depressed, sometimes for months, and only if you give them enough assistance will they be able to reach a stage of acceptance.

I have just worked with a patient who has gone through seven operative procedures for cancer including a colostomy and is now admitted for "palliative" radiation therapy. She is in a very depressed state and asked, "How would you feel if you were me?" What would your answer be?

I would most likely say to her that I would be very sad too.

The stages of dying seem to be analogous to those of the suddenly severely handicapped person. Do you have any comments on this concept?

This is true. A loss of any kind will provoke the same kind of adjustment reactions that we call "the stages of dying."

Do most dying patients lose the fight for life when they realize they are dying?

No.

What type of response do you make to a patient who asks, "Why should I? I'm going to die anyway and I wish I were dead"?

Many patients do not want to be pushed doing things they are not ready to do anymore. A patient who says, "I'm going to die anyway and I wish I were dead" has to be reevaluated. Maybe his suffering is too much for him to bear; maybe the pain relief is not adequate; maybe nobody really cares about him. A patient who has help—physical, psychological, and spiritual—is usually able to bear it and will be able to come out of his desperate plea "I wish I were dead." If all help is given and the patient still talks this way, I have said, "Yes, I can understand that."

What do you say to someone who says, "I'm no good to anybody. Why don't you just let me die?"

The fact that he talks to me proves that he is wrong because his sharing with me what he's going through will enable me to be a better physician to other terminally ill patients. I feel very comfortable saying that to such patients.

How do you respond to a terminal patient who says he doesn't want to get up because he's going to die anyway—what's the use?

Sometimes those patients are right. Often we expect too much from our critically ill patients. I have seen many critically ill children who were forced to attend school, to do things that pleased the grown-ups when the child, indeed, needed to decathect and wean off and wanted to be left in peace. It is important to differentiate between this kind of healthy weaning off on the part of the dying patient and a pathological depression where the patient is giving up hope prematurely and does not want to "bother anymore." With very depressed patients who have given up hope, it helps to let them talk about their sense of futility and hopelessness. With a patient who is in the process of separation, it is mandatory that we allow him to wean off in order to find his own inner resources and peace.

How do you respond to the dying patient who expresses concern for his loved one who will be left alone in this world after he dies?

I would empathize with him and would ask if there is anything I can do to make it easier for the ones he leaves behind. I would also see if he has finished his unfinished business, if he has written a will, if there are any other financial or other matters that have to be taken care of while he is still capable of doing so. If the family "limps behind" in the stages, I would see if they can receive some counseling to help them face the reality of the impending death.

THE END OF LIFE—HOPEFULLY ACCEPTANCE

Have we really been talking about death and dying or about life and living before death occurs? I suspect that reflection on the difference will be rewarding.

When I give lectures on death and dying and share with you what we have learned from our dying patients, it is very clear to me that these are lessons for the living. It is from our dying patients that we learn the true values of life, and if we could reach the stage of acceptance in our young age, we would live a much more meaningful life, appreciate small things, and have different values.

In talking to a dying loved one are you supposed to be honest about your feelings of fears, loss, separation? Can we really stop playing games?

Yes, we can. When I visited a dying woman lately with whom I was very close, I told her that in case this was my last visit I wanted her to know that I would miss her terribly. She blurted out, "I should hope so!" The moment she said that she apologized and I laughingly asked her if she really meant to be a phony in our last being together or if we hadn't learned long ago to be honest together. This was followed by a big embrace and we then talked very openly and frankly about what it was going to be like when she was no longer around. When I left, she said this was the best meeting we ever had together.

I have a patient with terminal cancer with complete bilateral block. Her husband requested, "Just keep her comfortable." We sedate her when she becomes rest-

less, otherwise she's quite lethargic from the uremia. She apparently has visual hallucinations, i.e., she has seen her deceased mother, a sister, her only son. She asks only to sleep and states she is going home on Tuesday. Psychologically I think I am prepared. Do you really believe she senses something we don't know?

I don't know if she senses something you don't know because you know that she is going to die soon, and if my guess is right, she will probably die on Tuesday. Patients know not only that they are dying, but many of our patients are able to convey to us when they are going to die and most of the time they are quite accurate. If she already relates to her late mother, deceased sister, and only son who died before her, it is very likely that she has already decathected and weaned herself off from the relationships in this world and is prepared to die.

Does the patient express a different sense of dignity when he resigns himself to his fate rather than accepting it?

Patients who are in the stage of acceptance show a very outstanding feeling of equanimity and peace. There is something very dignified about these patients, while people in the stage of resignation are very often indignant, full of bitterness and anguish, and very often express the statements, "What's the use"; "I'm tired of fighting." It's a feeling of futility, of uselessness and lack of peace which is quite easily distinguishable from a genuine stage of acceptance.

Are you implying that it makes no difference how you interpret the meaning of death for yourself and others so long as you have some way of interpreting it for yourself and that you feel at ease with it?

People see many different meanings in death. If they are at peace and comfortable with their own, I think that is the best we can hope for.

I have heard that at the end of a dying person's life, a summary of their whole life flashes before their eyes. Have you heard of this too?

Many of my dying patients have relived experiences from their past life. I think this is a period of time when the patient has switched off all external input, when he begins to wean off, when he becomes very introspective, when he tries to remember incidents and people important to him, and when he ruminates once more about his past life in an attempt to, perhaps, summarize the value of his life and to search for meaning. We found that little significant memories and moments with loved ones help the patient most in the very final stage of his life.

In the recent death of my mother I saw little or no decathexis as you described in your book. Was her separation from us too private for me to see?

It is possible that it was too private, but it is also possible that she was in peace and in a stage of acceptance and was so comfortable that she didn't need to separate gradually.

I have always wondered how a patient knows he is going to die within maybe the next half hour. Have you ever talked with a patient who has told you exactly what he felt in these last moments?

Many of our patients have been able to tell us the time of their dying. Innumerable patients have asked us to call family members or wanted to call in a favorite nurse to thank her. Many a patient has asked the nurse to comb his hair and put his new shirt on, to make him neat and clean. Then he asks to be left alone for a little while, and when we returned the patient had died. I think this is what we refer to as the psychophysiological cues that the patient picks up prior to his death.

You said that our goal is not to move the patient from one stage to another because they may need denial; yet you talk about the last stage as though it were a goal—especially with the example of the lady who pinched her husband's cheek. You suggested quite strongly that good counseling could move her to acceptance before her husband's death. Please explain this contradiction.

It may sound as if it were a contradiction and I think it's a matter of semantics. The ideal would be if both the dying patient and the patient's family could reach the stage of acceptance before death occurs. In that case there is little if any grief work to do though there is, naturally, grief in either case. It is not our goal, however, to push people from one stage to another. If the patient requires more time in a given stage or if he has no intention of really facing his finiteness, if he prefers to remain in the stage of denial, we do him a better service to allow him to stay in the stage of denial. If a patient has been angry all his life long or was a revolutionary or a fighter, it is much more likely that he will remain in the stage of anger until the moment he dies. If somebody has been a depressed personality and is filled with self-pity and remains this way at the end of his life, it is very unlikely that he will be cheerful and that he will accept his own dying with a smile on his face and a sense of equanimity. In these cases we should not push the patient to "behave in the manner that gratifies our need." We should be available to the patient, we should help him to move if and when *he* is ready to move; and without some additional help, some patients may have difficulties doing that.

How many patients, if any, have you encountered who have reached the last stage of acceptance at the time you had your interviews?

I think most of our patients would reach the stage of acceptance if it were not for the members of the helping professions, especially the physicians, who cannot accept the death of a patient. If we as physicians have the need to prolong life unnecessarily and to postpone death, the patient often regresses into the stage of depression and anger again and is unable to die in peace and acceptance. The second and quantitively more frequent problem is the immediate family which "hangs on" and cannot "let go." It is very difficult for a man to die with peace and equanimity if he sees the turmoil and pain he causes his wife who is not able to reach the stage of acceptance. If we see such a conspiracy of silence or such a discrepancy in the stages, the people to help are those who "limp behind in the stages." By this, I mean that we have to help the physician to face it or the wife to face it, and in an indirect way we will help the dying patient to either remain in the stage of acceptance or to reach it.

How incompatible is acceptance of death and the medically positive attitude of the will to live, to fight to stay alive and get better?

Acceptance of death is the most realistic thing that a person can work through since all of us have to die sooner or later. When a patient has accepted the reality of his own finiteness, then he has a much better chance to use all of his internal energies to help the physician and the treatment team fight to keep him alive. One does not rule out the other, but rather enhances the appreciation of life and the will to live.

My parents are over sixty years of age. All their good friends seem to be dying or dead. When I visit home, my mother talks about not wanting to get old and feeble. She receives gifts and says that I should have the gifts when she is dead. I don't know what to say to my parents about such matters.

I think you should understand that it is not very pleasant to be getting old and to be losing one's friends and relatives one by one. It is understandable that many people in our society do not want to get old because they do not have large families who can care for them when they are unable to attend to their own needs. It is not very enjoyable to spend the last years of your life in a nursing home. You can empathize with your mother and try to think now of what you would do if she reaches an old age. If you hear your mother's wishes now while she can still think clearly and while you can talk about it at a rather lengthy distance from her anticipated death, things will be much easier later on.

2

Special Forms of Communication

It is relatively easy to work with patients who can verbalize their needs, wishes, and feelings. We have, however, an increasing number of patients on respirators who are unable to speak. With the ever-increasing number of old people we will also be faced with more stroke patients, who survive but are unable to write a note or express their needs verbally. Those are the patients who need our very special attention. We will have to remember that they are often able to hear, feel a touch, and that they can also give us cues and signals which we have to receive and comprehend, if we are to maintain a meaningful and not just a mechanical relationship with them.

There are many languages the patient can use in communicating his needs to us. The very young ones "talk" to us in a *nonverbal symbolic language*, e.g., through drawings and in play. If a young patient shoots his very ill roommates down with an imagined pistol—while desperately waiting for a cadaver kidney for a transplant—he may express his urgent desire that his roommate hurry up and die so he may be the recipient of one of his kidneys. Perhaps the neediest group—usually older children and adolescents, but also adults who are afraid to die—use a *symbolic verbal language*. If a young terminally ill child, alone in a hospital room, inside an oxygen tent, asks her nurse, "What is going to happen when I am inside this oxygen tent and a fire breaks out?" she is really expressing her helplessness and fear of death. It is imperative that we train hospital personnel in these communications.

The patient's awareness of his body processes, sensed consciously or unconsciously, is very important. To give an example, a man who subsequently died on an operating room table of a brain tumor, when on Rorschach testing, showed repetitive percepts of smoldering, burning coal, and snow. This was his expression of his symbolic language.

I think it is important that we learn the symbolic language of our critically ill, terminally ill, and handicapped patients because they tell us a lot about the patient's own concepts of death and about his own awareness of what is happening in his body. The best example perhaps is drawings by children which sometimes show ahead of time when metastases begin to develop and we have to learn to read and interpret these drawings in order to be able to communicate to them.

How do you handle the patient who is near dying, but is unable to talk due to a stroke?

I try to talk to him anyway and give him symbols or signals for yes and no answers. If he is able to write, I let him write out his answers. There are many people who can learn to write with a pencil in their mouth or who can at least read with a talking book when they are no longer able to communicate verbally. All these tools have to be used with patients who are unable to verbalize normally.

How good is the psychological impact of nonverbal symbolic language on the dying patient? When do you know just how much to involve the family members in the patient's nonverbal symbolic language?

If a family is willing to learn the communications of the dying patient, especially the nonverbal symbolic language, I will give them all my time and attention teaching them how to "read" the patient and how to be better able to communicate.

How can you help an aphasic patient who is dying? How do you know what he is asking?

If he can write, try to talk with him and give him a piece of paper and pencil. If he cannot write any more, give him a symbol for yes and one for no. Try to have what we call a "monologue dialogue." You will be surprised how much you can converse with these patients if you take time, if you are patient, and if you don't give up too soon.

A "monologue dialogue" means that you anticipate his questions and ask him to respond with yes or no. If his answer is in the affirmative, you answer his question and then proceed until he gives you the signal that you answered all his questions.

If you can't use the types of languages that you mention, what else can you do to get someone to talk?

Sometimes it does not take a verbal language. Sometimes it just takes companionship and care. You do not desert people who are not ready to talk. If you simply sit with them and continue to show your care for them, they will occasionally open up without a word spoken on your part and will share with you their turmoil.

How do you translate the patient's and/or the family's symbolic language quickly enough to respond appropriately?

You don't always make the translation quickly enough, but if you have a family who is waiting outside of the room of the patient who is in the process of dying, sometimes you have to translate immediately because there is no tomorrow. The same thing is true of dying patients when the family is not present. In these cases I try to translate though I'm very often not sure, and very often I'm mistaken. The family or the patient knows that I've tried and if I don't respond correctly they will then try to rephrase what they are talking about.

How does one care for the patient who is critically ill in an intensive care or coronary care unit whose illness has been very sudden and acute?

This patient may be so critically ill that he is unable to communicate much with his environment or he may have a tracheotomy, or he may be hooked up on all sorts of equipment and so in one sense be handicapped because of these life-saving devices. It is important that we become aware of these patients' needs, of their, perhaps, eye communications, that we spend a little extra time sitting with them and trying to find their cues and trying to respond to them.

What do you do with patients who are semiconscious due to sedation?

I try to reduce the amount of sedatives so that he has moments when he is clear and is able to communicate with me about his needs. If you have no authority over the sedation, you should visit the patient when he is more alert, before he gets the next dosage.

Are there patients without a language? Just victims of our society?

I think there are many mute patients who are no longer using a language because they are so withdrawn and so lonely and so miserable that they have given up trying to cry out for help. We had one case of a woman who was lying, apparently semiconscious, in her room alone for weeks. Everybody expected her to die. She was never visited. However, when one of our music therapists simply walked into her room and sang and played the guitar, she suddenly opened her eyes and much to the surprise of everybody, started to sing. At the end of her song she had tears in her eyes and asked, "How in the world did you know that this is my favorite hymn?" Music is a much-neglected form of language and can be used with these patients in a very effective way.

How do you deal with the patients who aren't physically able to talk? Can nonverbal communications, i.e., hand-holding, be enough? I know that this is for the nursing staff, but how would you deal with the anxious visitor and/or family or nurses who stick to the "turn every two hours" routine? The comatose patient is a human being with all the rights that this implies. How do you relate to them?

I think if you have a patient who is physically unable to talk, he needs nonverbal communication and verbal communication. If he can still hear, you should talk to him, you should relate to him verbally, you should not treat him as though he had lost his facility of hearing too. If you have visitors or families who are nervous and anxious, maybe by your own action and example you can show them how comfortable and gratifying this kind of communication can be.

How does an intubated patient communicate his fear of dying to staff and how should the staff help this patient? What should we be listening for?

I think you look at his eyes. If his eyes express fear and anxiety, go to him and say, "Are you scared?" If he then blinks his eyes or nods his head, sit with him and ask him, "What are you so afraid of? Are you afraid of a, b, c, d?" and give him examples of what you can conceive that he might be afraid of. When he holds and presses your hands very vehemently to a certain answer, talk to him about that specific aspect of it and reassure him that someone will stay with him until he is able to overcome his fear and anxiety. One of the most beautiful examples of this is the account of Dr. Sharman in the Bulletin of the Menninger Foundation of May, 1972, where he describes a physician-patient who experienced this kind of anxiety because of dependence on a respirator. Another physician was able to help him by simply coming in and telling him that he would stay by the patient's side.

How can one deal with elderly patients who have hardening of the cerebral arteries (senility) and are, in most ways, incoherent of surrounding happenings?

You treat each of them like a newborn infant—you feed them, you keep them dry, warm, and comfortable, and touch them, talk to them exactly as you would do with a little baby. They are quite aware of warmth, love, and tenderness even though they may not be able to express their appreciation verbally.

Where can one get some information on symbolic language? What is the best source?

Nothing has been published yet on the symbolic verbal and nonverbal language that dying patients use. A set of teaching tapes is available on request from the author.

I am unclear about nonverbal symbolic language. Does this include the squeezing of the hand, the stiff posture of the woman surrounded by her husband's imaginary flowers in the hospital?

Yes, any communication that is not verbalized is a symbolic nonverbal language. If a patient who is unable to speak looks frightened, this is a nonverbal expression of his fears.

What should we do about the long-term unconscious terminal patient?

This is a difficult question. I don't know how to respond to it fairly. We can't go around killing people; I am totally opposed to mercy killing. I think we have to treat them in the best way we know without artificially prolonging life. I do not believe in keeping bodies functioning through all sorts of machines, but I do believe that an unconscious patient who has a chance to recuperate should get the best medical care in the world. It is important to know that comatose patients are often aware of their surroundings. They often respond to the touch of a caring person and they often tell you afterward that they were able to hear what the nurses talked about in their belief that the patient "can't hear them anyway."

How can you respond effectively to a person who obviously wants help but with whom you can't communicate because of a language barrier?

If the patient has only a foreign language or has difficulty expressing himself in English, see if you cannot contact a student from a local university who understands the language the patient speaks. With a little extra effort it is possible to get students to occasionally visit the patient who will then be able to communicate some of his basic needs.

Is it true that the last of our senses to fail in death is hearing and, if so, should a person who is with a dying person reassure him of the visitor's presence verbally? Is this a comfort or does it create anxiety?

I think it is a great comfort to know that somebody sits with you in your dying hours and holds your hand. The visitor doesn't have to sit there and talk incessantly. Simply say, "Your daughter is here with you. Can you hear me?" and hold the patient's hand and tell her all the things that you perhaps were too hesitant to tell her when she was well.

How do you know if the semicomatose or comatose patient dies in peace?

I don't know that unless I knew the patient before he was comatose.

If a patient is physically unable to speak, but seems to have something terribly important to say, how would you get at the thing the patient wants?

If you know the patient well enough you may have to spend hours with him and simply guess, giving him a signal for yes and no. If you cannot figure out what he wants, see if you can find a next-of-kin who knows the patient better and who may be able to detect what the patient's request is.

How can I help a patient who is very depressed, refuses to see members of her immediate family, becomes angry with the nursing personnel, and wants to die? How can she be reached? She is seventy-eight, diagnosis Parkinson's disease. She speaks a foreign language, therefore there is a language barrier. She has a very strong will.

I think an angry patient in this age group who refuses to see the family would make me suspicious that the family has not handled her hospitalization well or has shipped her off to a nursing home without discussing the matter with her. Try to get somebody who speaks her language but is not related to her. This patient may then be able to talk about her anger and may find a friend with whom she can relate better than with her next-of-kin. Somebody should also see the family so that they do not remain angry at her and then become full of guilt feelings later when she dies.

How can you handle the patient who is very near dying, but is unable to talk due to a stroke?

You simply sit with him and hold his hand.

Is it possible for a person in a coma to sense, even hear persons in the room?

Yes, this is often the case. It depends upon the depth of the coma.

How do you handle the dying patient's family when the patient is comatose?

We are available to them and answer questions and see that the whole family doesn't sit around the patient's bed waiting for him to die. This can go on for days, weeks, and sometimes months and you have to help the family to continue to live, for the youngsters to continue to date, to go to a movie if necessary, and to do all the things they had done ordinarily. If you cannot do that, the family becomes more and more exhausted, more and more resentful. They will then need help after death occurs, in part because of their anger, guilt, and resentment during this prolonged waiting period which has been too exhausting, both physically and emotionally.

What would you do with a very sick patient who is afraid to die and at the same time is depressed by his deformities if he should live? The deformities include amputation of the limbs.

You try to listen to his concerns about his deformities. Perhaps you can bring in other patients who have had amputations and who have been able to live and function successfully. I think nobody is a better therapist than another patient who has gone through the same kind of tragedy and has made a success out of his life.

How can I best help a thirty-year-old single woman express herself and her thoughts about death, providing she is ready. She speaks only German (so do I) and has right-handed paralysis and dysphagia.

She is lucky that she has a friend who speaks the same language. If you are not afraid to talk about it, you should be able to communicate with her if she gives you any clues that this is what she wants to talk about.

In communicating with a dying patient, do you communicate in the same kind of language he is using? For example, if he is communicating symbolically, do you communicate symbolically or do you translate to plain English?

I very often use the same language that the patient uses and only when I feel that he is ready to put it into plain English do I occasionally change to English. If he then does not use the same communication I go back to the symbolic language.

How does one learn to hear what is being said in symbolic communication, verbal or nonverbal? How can we learn to be better listeners, to hear beyond the words?

With time, patience, and some "masters" who allow you to go with them, to sit with them at the bedside, and to observe what other perhaps more experienced people do in this area.

How do you know when it is advisable to enter into the patient's symbolic language system rather than communicating strictly in plain English?

When a patient uses a symbolic nonverbal language rather than plain English, it usually means that he is not yet ready to verbalize in English. If I feel he is almost ready to talk about it, I often use the technique of talking aloud to myself or a third person in the room and saying, "I wonder if he is talking about his final hours." The patient then says, "Oh yes, that's what I am talking about. My days are certainly counted," and he proceeds, then, in plain English. If he does not pick it up, I will continue in his own symbolic language.

How can you be sure that the patient is speaking symbolically and that your interpretation does not arise out of your own needs?

If I communicate with a patient and the patient responds positively, I presume that I made the right interpretation. In order to assure that we are not doing this work out of our own needs or to simply gratify our needs, we have a good interdisciplinary team who keeps an eye on each other and if somebody gets overinvolved or becomes nontherapeutic, we are open and frank enough to correct each other.

What communications can be given to a person who is a stroke patient and is critically ill and yet cannot convey verbally her fear of dying?

I would sit with her, stroke her hair, and say simply, "It's tough, isn't it?" You can then read in her looks or if she tries to hold your hand tighter whether she's scared or comfortable. This is a nonverbal communication on her part yet you are able to converse with her verbally.

How do you translate the patient's and/or the family's symbolic language quickly enough to respond appropriately? Do they tend to say some things more frequently than others?

This is almost exclusively a question of experience. We still make many mistakes, and are often unable to make the right interpretation, but I truly believe that it is better to try and make a mistake than not to try at all.

How do you know that your observations of nonverbal communication are correct without pushing the patients to voice their feelings?

I think if a patient responds favorably and positively you know that your observations were correct. You don't push patients if they do not want to express any feelings. They are the first ones to let you know verbally or nonverbally if you are too "pushy."

3

Suicide and Terminal Illness

Many professionals are afraid to tell their patients that they have a serious illness, out of a fear that the patients might contemplate suicide if they knew the truth. We cannot confirm this belief. Patients who are told gently that they are seriously ill and who are given hope simultaneously are able to handle the bad news with more courage than we usually give them credit for.

Patients who do consider suicide fall into different categories:

(1) Those who have a strong need to be in control of everything and everybody.

(2) Those who are told cruelly that they have a malignancy and "there is nothing else we can do for you because you came too late for help."

(3) Patients in the dialyses programs and/or potential organ-transplant patients who have been given too much hope and an unrealistic assessment of their condition, have a tendency to suddenly give up hope and often die of what we call a "passive suicide."

(4) Those patients who are neglected, isolated, and deserted, and receive inadequate medical, emotional, or spiritual help in this crisis.

The last group of terminally ill patients who may take their own lives are those who are usually not conventionally religious, but have accepted their finiteness and would rather shorten the process of dying than linger on for another few weeks or months in what they regard as useless suffering.

Are some patients "poor risks" (suicidal) for facing the reality of death?

Yes, there are people who always live as if there is a tomorrow, who have never faced any serious tragedies or loss in their life, who have never contemplated their death. When these patients are hit with a sudden tragedy which threatens their very existence, they may either go into a severe, deep depression or they may try to find refuge in a massive denial which makes treatment, discussion, and management of the prognosis extremely difficult. Some patients have to be in control all the time, and when they are faced with a terminal illness they feel that they have lost control. One way of regaining control is then to consider suicide. There are a few "techniques" which are extremely helpful with this last type of patient. Any procedure that the nurse or the physician has to do should be discussed ahead of time with the patient. He should be given the option of having this procedure done in the morning or in the afternoon. In this manner he gets a choice and is in control at least of the timing of certain procedures. And his family can call him up ahead of time and ask if he would like to have a visitor at a certain time or later on. This again gives him a feeling that he is in control of when he has his visitors. Many times patients improve rapidly through a small manipulation of the environment. This is done quite consciously to give the patient the feeling that he is still considered an

important human being. He should be allowed to make
as many decisions as technically possible.

*In the few instances that the cancer patient actually
does take his own life, is it usually when he first
learns he has cancer and is not yet seriously or pain-
fully ill?*

We have not heard of many cases where the patient
has attempted to take his life or actually committed
suicide in the early stages of a malignancy. It happens much more often at the end stage of his illness
when he is no longer able to care for himself, when the
pain becomes unbearable, and the expenses are so
high that he is beginning to get worried about his
family and contemplates suicide in order to shorten
the agony and decrease the bills for the family that he
leaves behind.

*Do you feel that people who commit suicide are deny-
ing death or accepting death?*

It can be either.

*The suicidal patient gives symbolic hints of his intent.
Does the "helping" person approach this patient dif-
ferently from the person who has a premonition of
impending death or the one who is terminally ill?*

I think the suicidal patient who is not terminally ill
gives symbolic hints of his intent. He asks for help and
you should be open and frank with him and offer your
help in any way possible to prevent this suicide.

What about suicide and the terminally ill patient?

We have had extremely few suicidal attempts among
our over eight-hundred terminally ill patients. The

group that has perhaps the highest mortality through suicide are those who are on dialysis or awaiting an organ transplant. They are much limited in their functioning, although they originally have high hopes for an organ transplant. When the transplant is not forthcoming or complications set in, they very often give up all hope and then become highly suicidal. They often commit what we call a "passive suicide": they break the rules, they may drink a lot of fluids, they may not take the medication, and in that manner, semipassively promote their death rather than take an overdose of medication.

Have you had suicidal terminally ill patients? If so, how did you handle the situation?

If a terminally ill patient contemplates suicide and talks with me about it I ask what about his present situation makes the continuation of life unbearable. If it is too much pain then we have to change the pain medication so that the patient is comfortable. If his family has deserted him we try to get the family reinvolved. If this is impossible we try to replace the family by our frequent visits and by trying to find a foster family, perhaps through a volunteer who has been trained in the care of dying patients and who loves this kind of work. We do everything humanly possible to help the patient to live life until he dies of natural causes. In all these years, in which we were able to take care of the physical, emotional, and spiritual needs of the patient, we have had only one suicide. If a ward has several suicides among its terminally ill patients, the staff should reevaluate the management of their patients.

*For one who desires death, how do you give the "will
to live," for example, to a suicidal patient or one who
is abusing himself with drugs or alcohol, so that he
will want to live and appreciate a useful life again?*

I think the first thing is not to be judgmental with
this kind of patient. You accept them the way they are
and try to find out why they are abusing themselves
with drugs or alcohol or no longer have a will to live.
Only then can you truly help them. These patients
naturally require professional help.

*Do you believe that a person has the right to take his
own life during a terminal illness, or do we have the
right to prevent this act?*

Our goal should be not to take lives but to help people to live until they die their natural deaths. If a
patient is deeply depressed and wants to end his life
we must first try to help him out of this depression. If
a terminally ill patient has accepted his own finiteness
and has put his house in order and then wants to
terminate his life, we cannot prevent it and we should
not judge his decision. But as long as such a patient is
in our care we should do our utmost to make his life
bearable, if not meaningful, so he is able to hold out
until his natural death.

*How can one help the family and friends to accept the
death of a person who has committed suicide?*

Those families and friends have to go through all
the stages of dying after death occurs. Because of the
nature of the death of this loved person, there are
usually a lot of additional guilt feelings and regrets.
It often requires professional help for the family to

reach the stage of peace and acceptance. This grief will naturally last much longer than if the person had died of natural causes.

What do you say to a patient who asks for mercy killing from a medical staff or threatens suicide by refusing to take his medication?

I don't think you can force a patient to take medication. If a patient refuses dialysis, further treatment, or medication, I think we have to accept that he has a right to dispose of his own body if he is mentally competent. If he is in a psychotic depression, I would regard it as my duty to help him out of this state. If he still refuses treatment or medication, I will accept his decision. If a patient asks for mercy killing, I would like to know why he asks for this. If he receives adequate pain relief, good physical, emotional, and spiritual help, a patient would ask for mercy killing only in extremely rare cases—perhaps one in a thousand. It is not our role to kill but to help people to live until they die. I am totally opposed to any form of mercy killing and I would play no part in it.

Do you believe that patients who are planning a suicidal death go through the reactive and silent grief type of depression?

I believe that patients who contemplate suicide slowly and consciously go through the same preparatory grief. There are naturally suicides where patients do not go through the stages of dying. These are usually people who are under the influence of drugs or alcohol and cannot think clearly. Also, psychotic patients who commit suicide do this for a reason different from that of non-psychotic patients.

Could suicide ever be a normal ending of the last stage of dying, that is, after full acceptance, perhaps to avoid suffering or liability, or is suicide always abnormal behavior?

No, I don't think suicide is always abnormal behavior. We have heard of patients who have completed their unfinished business, who have put their houses in order, have reached a stage of peace and acceptance, and have then terminated their lives, perhaps to leave a home and some money for a wife and children, or because they could not see any sense in prolongation of the dying process when they were ready to die.

What is so wrong with a person's committing suicide, if that's his way of keeping control?

In this work with terminally ill patients, we have learned not to be judgmental. It is not a question of right or wrong when a person considers suicide; for us it is a question of why this person wants to commit suicide. Where does this tremendous need come from, to be in control even of the time and way of one's death? If a patient is not afraid of death and dying, he is then able to give up this control and wait for his natural death. It requires very little counseling in order to achieve this with most patients.

Should suicide be everyone's right? If so, what limitations or parameters should there be as to the time and place and means?

I don't think we should advertise suicide as being everyone's right. There was a time in the history of France when suicide was regarded as the norm. There were certain "health stations" where poison was obtainable by people who wanted to commit suicide. I don't believe in mercy killing or in public facilitation of suicide. I think our role should always be to prolong a meaningful, functioning life and people should get all the help available in order to live meaningfully and spend their time and energy to live and not to contemplate suicide. If a terminally ill patient who is "beyond medical help" contemplates suicide by simply stopping the intake of medication or refuses additional medical help, I think he has a right to do so. I am fully aware that this includes my own judgment and my own differentiation between a patient's right to die his own death, to prevent an additional artificial prolongation of life on the one hand and the actual taking of one's own life on the other.

Do suicidal patients go through the same preparatory stages of death that terminally ill patients go through?

I think a certain number of suicidal patients go through the same stages. I would think this is true of the neurotic patient who is in a long chronic depression and has time to consciously and slowly consider the termination of his life. This would not be true for the spontaneous suicidal impulses of psychotic patients, nor would it be true of patients who commit suicide under the influence of drugs.

What are your views of suicide among the adolescent population, those who are essentially physically healthy individuals but have emotional problems?

They naturally need psychiatric help, and the parents should be included.

4

Sudden Death

The sudden, unexpected death of a loved one is a most tragic experience. In our death-denying society we are ill-prepared to handle the loss of a member of our family when there is no illness preparing us slowly for this eventual outcome.

It is of utmost importance that we assist a bereaved family to avoid irreparable trauma and endless suffering. Too many people, not given enough help, either go through years of unresolved grief or require psychiatric help later.

How can we help families whose relatives die quickly or violently with no time to go through the preparatory stages?

They have to be given enough time to get out of the state of shock and denial and they will have to go through all the stages after death occurs.

How can we help a patient who has recovered from a severe coronary overcome the fear of sudden death?

Many patients who have had a massive coronary and recovered become overanxious and are always afraid of another heart attack and sudden death. Those patients need some counseling to alleviate their anxiety and help them exercise, perhaps use a bicycle, so that they can live as much of a normal functioning life as their physician allows. Many of these patients are so tense and anxious all the time that the possibility of another coronary is much higher than if they are able, often through the help of professional counseling, to exercise and to live as normal a life as possible.

How can the family accept the sudden death of a child?

Nothing is more difficult than having to accept the death of a child. If it is a sudden death, and the child's family has had no preparation, this family sometimes needs years of working through the grief. This means that you should not desert these families but be available to them for months and months after the death of a child, while the parents and siblings go through the stages of dying after the death of the child.

What can we say and how can we be helpful in the event of sudden death several hours after an accident or a very unexpected death after a sudden severe illness?

In the few hours immediately after such an unexpected death, we cannot do much for the family except to remain available to them and help with the mechanical things that have to be done following a death. Most of these family members will be in a state of shock and denial. They need someone who can think clearly and unemotionally to notify the next-of-kin and make the funeral arrangements.

How do you handle the dying patient when the person she related to the most dies?

Death of an important figure during the dying process of a patient is one of the most difficult things that we have to face. In a hospital, where we interviewed about eight hundred terminally ill patients, one death is perhaps outstanding and was one of the most traumatic experiences of my life. This was the death of the most significant surgeon and physician who took care of many of my cancer patients. He died unexpectedly of a coronary one morning just prior to making rounds. Many of his patients who trusted him implicitly and explicitly and who loved him dearly were in the stage of tremendous shock and extreme anguish. Several of them preferred not to have any additional surgery since they regarded it as a sign that any further surgery would no longer be necessary. They go through a tremendous amount of grief over the loss of such a significant person. All of our patients required counseling in order to come to grips with the death of an important caring human being. The same thing holds true, naturally, if the husband of a terminally ill woman dies or a terminally ill patient loses a child during his or her hospitalization. They should be told the facts; the truth should not be withheld from them simply because they are terminally ill. Somebody has to take the time, share that news with them, and then remain available for helping them to work through this tremendous loss.

How do you handle the family of a person who has died in an accident when they come to the emergency room after death has occurred?

It is very important that the physician notify the family of the death of their relative and that this duty not be delegated to a nurse or member of another helping profession. It is not that the nurse cannot handle it, sometimes she can handle it more appropriately, but for the family it is important to know that the physician was present, that everything possible was tried to prevent the death. If a physician is nowhere in sight, the family believes that the physician was not available when help might still have been given. This notification of death should not be done by telephone, or in a hallway, or the emergency room. It should be done in a small, quiet "screaming room," adjacent to the emergency room, where the family can sit down, perhaps have a cup of coffee or a soda. There the physician spends a few minutes with them and answers questions. The physician will then have to resume his work, but another member of a helping profession, preferably a member of the clergy, a social worker, a nurse, or a trained volunteer, should stay with the family until they are emotionally and physically ready to leave the hospital. Family members should not be sedated, but should be allowed to cry, to scream, to pray, to curse or ventilate their feelings in whatever way they choose. These families will often be in a state of shock or anger. This should be accepted and a volunteer may sometimes have to take them home. The same helping person who has been in the "screaming room" with them at the time of death should call the family four weeks afterward and invite them to return to the hospital if they want to talk about the incident once more. The family members usually welcome such a discussion full-heartedly. They will then ask the questions they were emotionally not ready to ask at the time of the great shock. Many of them will ask, "Did he open his eyes once more?"; "Did he mention my name?"; "Was he conscious when he arrived?" If these answers can be given, the family will appreciate this confrontation with the reality of death. It is often after this second meeting that the family begins to work through the grief and the mourning process.

What about sudden death? How do you help the family to accept this?

When a family is faced with a sudden accidental death it is important that we do not prevent them from viewing the body. Patients who have committed suicide or accident victims are often quite mutilated and the hospital personnel prevents the family from viewing the body. This causes a lot of psychological problems for the survivors. It is important that the nurses prepare the body in an acceptable fashion so that the family can view at least part of an identifiable body in order to face the reality of the death. If we prevent the family from seeing the body, they may remain in the stage of denial for years to come and never quite face the reality of the death.

How can one best help a family who has experienced a sudden violent death, if there are many guilt feelings and massive defense mechanisms so that the subject of death is avoided?

With time and patience you may be able to help this family talk about it. Some of these families remain in the stage of denial for months and sometimes years to come and need professional help to accept such a death.

When a child comes to the hospital for minor surgery and child and parents are well prepared, who helps the family when a sudden and unexpected death occurs (due to anesthesia, bleeding, etc.)? Everybody is usually in a state of shock, including the treatment team. How can the staff help the family when the staff is equally ill-prepared and did not expect this to happen?

We, the staff, have to take the time out to sit together and discuss the situation and our feelings openly and honestly, even if it means we cry together. A staff member who was not directly involved in the care of the deceased patient would be in the best position to help others who were closely affiliated with the patient. Only if we as care-taking persons have been able to sort out our own feelings are we then able to help the family through this crisis.

When there is a sudden death, there is a mandatory requirement for an autopsy. Many relatives regard this as an additional insult to the deceased (they say, "He has suffered enough"), and are extremely upset that they cannot prevent this. How can we help them?

We should explain to them that the autopsy will be done with utmost care and dignity, not unlike a surgical procedure. Information gained may shed light on the cause of death and alleviate any guilt or doubt that

we have done everything possible in the present state
of medical knowledge.

*How do we help parents of a baby who died through
so-called crib-death?*

We reassure them first that they are not guilty of
neglect, that we do not yet know the exact cause of
this sudden death. We also refer them to the SID—
the Sudden Infant Death National Foundation—an
organization of parents who have gone through this
experience themselves and may be better able to help
this family.

*When a patient arrives dead on the ramp of our emer-
gency room, the driver is often advised to take the body
directly to the morgue, so we don't have to "bother"
with it. When the family arrives a few minutes later
they have no opportunity to see the body and are left
without any assistance. I, as a nurse, feel very bad
about this and usually avoid these situations. There must
be a way to handle this situation in a more human
fashion.*

The fact that you feel bad about it gives me some
hope that such cruel practices are on the way out. It
may be "easier" for the staff to handle the situation in
this manner, and avoid the whole issue, but it surely
leads to a lot of heartache, bitterness, resentment, and
unresolved grief. There should be a place where the
body can be viewed, where the family can recuperate
from the initial shock, where there is a telephone, a
bathroom, a cup of coffee available, and where they
can sit silently and not be rushed out. If people like
you, who obviously has some empathy, could stay with
them, it would be of great help and reassurance in the

kindness of men! Nobody should be sent around from place to place in search of a body which is shielded from them.

When a patient has just died, the relatives are asked to come into the room. Some of them actually talk to the deceased, touch him or even kiss him. Don't you think this is morbid?

No, I don't think this is morbid. I am much more concerned about people who appear very stoic, calm, detached, and outwardly very composed; those who do not say a word or shed a tear; those who are afraid to even look at the body and quietly leave the room. They will eventually have a delayed reaction which may be worse.

Sometimes a mutilated patient is brought into our emergency room and dies shortly after. Many staff people are quite angry and judgmental about the chaplain, who is ill at ease when we expect him to console the family. What can I, as a nurse, do to help him?

You can tell him that you appreciate how tough it must be for him. He is a man of God and we expect them to have all the answers. This is very unfair. We have to understand that they have problems, too. They know that God is loving and in command of all things and they often can not comprehend themselves why such a tragedy has happened. It is very painful for them to be reassuring and consoling when they too ask "Why?" Tell him to try a silent holding-hand approach next time—it may mean more than any words spoken. And you can do the same for him!

Patients who die within a short time after arrival in the hospital receive all sorts of life-saving procedures such as infusions and resuscitative attempts. My question is whether we should remove all the equipment before the family is allowed to come into the room. Sometimes I wonder if it would not be better to leave them in the room in order to "prove" that we have really tried. I must say that this concern comes from experiences with families who questioned us as to why we did not even try when their relative was brought in dead on arrival and beyond any help.

My first reaction to your question is: To whom do you need to prove that you did everything possible, to yourself or the family? I believe that we should clean up the body, cover all mutilated parts, air out the room, take the infusions out of the arm but leave the equipment in the room.

I am a social worker and just had a terrible experience. A whole family was in an accident; the mother was killed, the father is in a coma, and one of the children died shortly after arrival in the hospital. Two school-children are left on the ward in fairly good physical condition. They ask about their parents but I was told not to tell them anything until the grandparents arrive from out of town. The way they looked at me, I know that they know. What can I do?

Sit with them and tell them that you just visited their daddy. Tell them that he cannot come to visit them at this time but their grandparents are on the way. Tell them where they can reach you when they have questions. If they ask about their mother you have to tell them the truth.

*Sometimes, especially in very ill patients who antici-
pate cardiac surgery, they know they will die on the
table or during the postoperative period. To what can
this be attributed? How do they know?*

Not only patients who undergo surgery or terminally
ill patients, but also many of our patients whom we
regarded as doing relatively well have told us of their
awareness of their own impending death. Most of the
time they were correct. What kind of psychophysiological cues they pick up we are not sure, but we do know
that patients are aware of their impending death and
that they do need someone to talk to who does not
laugh at them, who does not belittle them, and who
does not try to talk them out of it.

*Do the stages of death also pertain to those who die
through trauma?*

A patient who is in an accident and then dies an
hour later does not have the time to work through the
stages of dying. Most of these patients will die in the
stage of shock and denial or sometimes anger.

*What emotional support can you give to a woman who
loses her baby at birth or shortly afterward?*

The loss of a child is one of the most difficult things
to accept. You give the woman your presence, your
care, and your empathy and you try to be available to
her in her time of loneliness and emptiness and she
will be grateful for it. Time will be required to come
to grips with a loss of any child.

What emotional support can you give to the family of persons who die suddenly?

A patient who is brought into the emergency room and dies within minutes or hours is usually surrounded by members of the helping profession working to save or prolong the patient's life. The family is often left totally alone; nobody has time to relate to them; they are often not allowed to be with a critically injured relative until after death occurs, and they are often in the stage of numbness, shock, or denial, or in an often justified stage of rage at being deprived of the last few minutes with a loved one while he was still alive and would have been aware of their presence. The help you can give these families is to take them into a screaming room to help them cry, curse, pray, or express whatever feelings they need to express. Do not sedate those relatives and do not try to rush them into signing papers and getting them out of the hospital as fast as possible. Every emergency room should have a room nearby where a counselor, therapist, chaplain, or a trained volunteer can stay with these family members until they are ready to leave the hospital. If you call these relatives a month later and ask them if they would like to have a return visit to talk about it, they would be very grateful and they will then rehash the whole scene once more to make it real. Then they are able to work through the stages of dying as we have outlined earlier.

Do families go through the same grieving process when a member is killed suddenly and unexpectedly as when there is a chronic illness?

Yes, except the bargaining is often eliminated and the grief process may last longer because they have been so totally unprepared.

How can we help the individual or the family of an individual who is thrust from a happy, healthy life into the sudden prospect of death due to severe injury or acute illness? Is there time for the "stages"?

People who have sudden tragedies and who have a very short time between the onset of an acute illness and their actual death often remain in a state of shock and denial. Some patients pass to a stage of anger; others are in a mixture of shock, denial, bargaining, anger, and depression. One of our patients who had only two weeks between his hospitalization and his death was able to pass through all the stages and reach the stage of acceptance. I think it is important to emphasize that our goal should not be to help people through the five stages and reach the stage of acceptance. The outline of these five stages is only the common denominator that we found in most of our terminally ill patients. Many do not flow from stage one to five in a chronological order, and this is totally irrelevant to their well-being. Our goal should be to elicit the patient's needs, to find out where *he* is, and then to see what form and manner we can help him best, no matter how much time he has between his illness or accident and his actual death. In other words, if a patient is more comfortable remaining in the stage of denial, we will not naturally, tear this denial down, and we will treat him with the same attention and care as we would if he were in the stage of acceptance. If somebody has been angry all his life long, he's more likely to die in the stage of anger because this is more in character and according to his previous life-style. If we try to sedate him and make him "nice, quiet, and peaceful" we gratify our needs and not the patient's needs!

Could you make some statements from your experience about coping with sudden death? What kind of approaches are most helpful in dealing with the patient and his family?

Sudden deaths are not handled well in general. We attempt to sedate the family when they come into the emergency room, have them sign papers as fast as possible, and get them out of the hospital as soon as possible. This does not help the family to face the reality of a sudden and unexpected death. It often leaves them in the stage of numbness, shock, and denial; occasionally in the stage of rage and anger in which they displace their anger onto the ambulance driver or the physician in the emergency room. We have found it most helpful to have a quiet room adjacent to the emergency room where a trained volunteer, a chaplain, a nurse, or other member of a helping profession can be available to these families. There the family can cry, or question, or express their anguish and their grief. In the meantime, the body of the deceased person should be prepared in as acceptable a condition as possible in order to help the family view the body, which makes a future working through of grief more realistic. We found that the counseling that has to follow a sudden death is not meaningful in the first few weeks. If the member of the helping profession who has been present during the tragedy could contact the family four weeks after death and invite them to come back to the emergency room to "talk about it once more," the family will then be able to ask the questions that were never raised while they were in the state of shock and denial. For example, "Did he open his eyes once more?"; "Was he conscious?"; "Did he mention my name?"; "Did somebody stay with him and hold his hand?" If this can be done four weeks after death, the family will then proceed to work through their own grief, which may last from a few months to several years.

How can you alleviate the fear of dying of patients who are about to undergo surgery such as open heart surgery where they have a 50-50 chance of living? How can you lessen the guilt of the members of the family who have motivated the patient to undergo such delicate surgery, especially when the patient dies?

When the patient has to undergo surgery, especially heart surgery with a 50-50 chance, there has to be enough time prior to surgery to discuss all the pros and cons of the surgery with the patient, to answer questions that he may have. If he has any strong, ambivalent, or negative feelings about the surgery they should be discussed prior to the operation. If a family pushes a patient into surgery and the patient does not survive, they naturally have a tremendous amount of guilt and often require counseling afterward to help them alleviate it. Again, I think a careful and sometimes time-consuming preparation prior to surgery, not only for the patient, but for the family, is mandatory in order to avoid much suffering, physically and emotionally, after the operation.

5

Prolongation of Life

Terminally ill patients pose many problems to us during the course of their illness, perhaps the greatest come during the very end of their suffering. There is a point of no return, no chance of ever getting up again or of resuming any form of functioning existence. The patient may exist this way for weeks or months. When are we serving him better by doing less? Who decides when life-prolonging measures should be stopped? Who decides what ordinary or extraordinary means are? Do we have a right to shorten a life, no matter how meaningless to us?

These are the questions that come up in every workshop, in every seminar, on the care of the dying patient. As Erich Fromm says: "I think there is no such thing as medical ethics. There are only universal human ethics applied to specific human situations." It is this humanistic conscience, referring to the philosophic or religious humanistic tradition, which has to be our guide in every difficult case. We always have to put ourselves into the situation of the patient *first*, then consider the family and the staff's needs, because all of these will play a role in our final decision.

We should also find a new definition for "euthanasia" since it is used for "good death" (*e.g.*, the patient's own natural death without prolonging his dying process unduly), and for mercy killing, which has nothing to do with the original intent of the word euthanasia. To me this is the difference between allowing someone to die his own death or killing him. I am naturally in favor of the former and opposed to the latter.

But real situations are not that simple. There are many borderline cases where we truly wonder whether we should keep a nasal tube or an I.V. going or whether we are only prolonging the terminal suffering by a few more weeks or months. The most beautiful hospital for the care of such patients is probably the St. Christopher Hospice in London, under the directorship of Dr. Cecily Saunders. Her patients, most of them with terminal cancer, are kept comfortable with adequate pain-relief; no mechanical means or machines are used in the Hospice; and neither food nor visitor restrictions are known for those patients. The questions so often raised in this country do not occur in the British Hospice, simply because they apply "the true art of medicine" to every patient. They surround them with love, faith, and excellent medical-emotional support, which allows the patient to live until he dies. The Rose Hawthorne Hospital in Fall River, Massachusetts is a similar though smaller facility.

Why do we try to keep patients alive with "horrible diets and treatments" when we know death is very near?

We very often keep "patients alive with horrible diets and treatments," because we hope that such treatment will bring about a remission and the patient will be able to live a fairly normal existence for another few months or years. If a patient is full of cancer, and we have a new chemotherapy available, we may be tempted to use this new treatment in the hope of making the patient more comfortable and to delay his death. It is also used in order to find out if a certain cancer responds to the new treatment, and if it does we may be able to use it on other patients later on in an earlier stage of their cancer. It is sometimes difficult to say whether or not the side effects and the added restrictions are more difficult and painful than the natural disease. It is sometimes questionable whether these treatments are really for the benefit of the patient or are used for our own needs and because of our own inability to accept the patient's death.

What are your views on euthanasia?

I am totally opposed to any kind of mercy killing, but I am in favor of allowing the patient to die his or her own death, without artificially prolonging the dying process.

Does society have the right to keep alive those who are designated by fate or God to die? Aren't we playing God? What are your feelings on this?

I don't think we should keep people artificially alive when they are no longer functioning human beings. This may be playing God, but I think it is a duty of every physician to keep somebody alive in a functioning condition. God may have given the physician the wisdom and the knowledge to do this. I'm very opposed to keeping people alive who are functioning purely as organ systems due to some equipment that is hooked up to them.

What about a patient who dies on you? When do you try to resuscitate?

If there is any chance for a meaningful life with some degree of functioning and at least the ability to express and receive expressions of human feelings, you should resuscitate by all means. If a cancer-ridden patient is dying on you I would not resuscitate.

Is it a patient's right to decide when to turn off the machines?

Yes, it should be the patient's privilege to decide when he is no longer willing to go along with a certain extension of life which to him may not only be meaningless, but also very costly.

Is euthanasia ever legal in the United States?

There are as yet no statutes legalizing euthanasia, but the trend is in that direction. It is important to differentiate between euthanasia as the word was used in the past, when it meant a good death, and as it is now used to designate mercy killing, which I personally cannot ever see as a good death. I am in favor of allowing patients to die their own natural deaths, without undue prolongation of the dying process and prolonged suffering, but I am not in favor of giving patients an overdose to "relieve them of their suffering."

Regarding President Truman's death—would you comment on the public's feeling that these people belong to the public and their lives should be prolonged (against their personal wishes) because of an "obligation" to the public to keep them alive?

It is tragic that people in such exposed positions often have to suffer more. It is inhuman and inexcusable when we prolong the dying process to such an extent as President Truman and Eleanor Roosevelt had to suffer. The doctors certainly do it in good faith, but it is not in the service of the patient.

What are your thoughts about keeping people alive with machines in hospitals when they are terminally ill or have only a very slim chance of getting better?

I think any patient who has a chance of getting better should get all the technical assistance that we have available. Patients who are beyond medical help and whose organs are kept functioning only with machines are not benefiting from this kind of management, and we should have the courage to learn when to call it quits.

If the patient is unable to decide whether extraordinary means to prolong life are to be used then who is responsible? What happens when family members cannot agree?

The patient should always have the first voice. If the patient is in a coma, or if he is not of legal age, the family's opinion is usually considered next. If the family cannot agree (and in the case of children, their parents should not be asked to make such a horrible decision), a treatment team should meet and make the decision as a group. Our ideal treatment team includes the physician who treats the patient, any specialist who has been in on the case, a member of the clergy, the nurses, the social worker, and a consulting psychiatrist. This team should understand the needs not only of the dying patient, but also of his family. In the case of children we ask each other if we would continue treatment if this were our child? If the unanimous opinion is against any use of extraordinary means, we then present this decision to the family. We do not ask them for an opinion, but simply state our decision, adding that it would require a strong veto on their part to make us decide otherwise. In a case when the child died, the family did not have feelings of guilt to add to grief, nor the thought, "Maybe if we had added another treatment, Susie would still be alive." They thus have the opportunity to blame us for the death of the child when they are in the stage of anguish and anger. With comatose patients when the family cannot agree, we try to make a group decision, involving not only the professional team, but also members of the family.

Will you speak briefly about your attitude toward physicians who, by prolonging life by exclusively artificial means, refuse to allow patients to die?

These are the physicians who have been trained to cure, to treat, to prolong life, and who have never had any instruction on how to be a physician to terminally ill patients. They have been trained to regard dying patients as a failure. They themselves usually have unresolved fears of death and they feel uncomfortable when "a patient dies on them." It takes understanding, patience, and communication to make these physicians aware that they are not helping the patient, nor do they resolve their own internal conflicts by these procedures.

*Is it possible, when a person reaches a point of accept-
ance that he is to die soon, that he can no longer
accept the fact that he can mentally overcome his
physical disease, to allow him to die and not extend
his life just for the sake of keeping him alive? This is
his wish, to be allowed to die. How does one overcome
the fear of how one will behave and not lose one's
dignity when terminally ill? Also, the fear of being a
burden on everyone else?*

Many patients have reached their stage of acceptance, have expressed the wish to be allowed to die,
and have been able to keep their equanimity and their
dignity to the very end. If the patient's needs are
respected, if he has been truly loved, he will not be
afraid of being a burden to everyone else.

*What would you do and how would you respond to a
friend who lived in terror of a crippling stroke and
could not rest unless assured that he would be merci-
fully put out of his misery if he became too helpless
physically or mentally to end his own life?*

I would not promise him that I would put him out
of his misery, because I would not be able to do that.
I could only promise him that I would help him to live
until he dies, in spite of his limitations.

*How does one help people who are ashamed of liv-
ing, who think they do not deserve to live, because
they may be different in some way? Also—in view of
the overpopulation problem—does one have the right
to allow sick people to die by denying them medicine?*

I think people who are ashamed to live because of a
handicap, or because they are different in some way,

need professional help. This world has enough room, and should have enough love to accept people who are different no matter in what way. Overpopulation should never be a reason for helping people to die by denying them medication or through any other means. If we did this, we would soon end up in another Nazi society.

How do you deal with a family who wants the life of a patient prolonged, but the patient would like to be allowed to die?

This happens many, many times. It means that the patient has reached the stage of acceptance, but the family is behind in the stages of dying, maybe in the stage of denial, anger, or bargaining. In these cases, you spend all your time and effort on the family and help them work through their unfinished business, so that they can allow the patient to die, to "let go."

Do you believe in prolonging death by giving I.V. feedings when a patient is already unconscious and in a coma?

I think it depends a great deal on the patient. I have seen many unconscious patients who were in comas and were given intravenous feedings, and who are now walking around, healthy, happy, and functioning. If a patient has been unconscious and in a deep coma for a long time, I think his brain waves must be checked repeatedly to see if he is still really alive, or only kept "alive" by a machine. In the latter case, I would naturally stop the intravenous feedings.

You referred to the ping-pong game of deciding where the patient may die—at home, as he wants, or in a hospital, which is a costly workshop for the medical profession, where his life can be extended through intravenous and other means. Should we the medical professionals extend the life of the vegetating person? Wouldn't it be merciful to let him die? President Truman's case is a good example of this.

Yes, I think there is still too much ambivalence in most of us, not only as to where a patient may die, but also as to where to keep some of our difficult patients. We should ask the patient if he would prefer to return home or if he would prefer to stay in the hospital, where the care may be a bit easier than at home, especially now when there is usually a lack of visiting nurses, physicians who make house calls, or people to take care of the night watch, etc. If the family gets enough assistance, I think most patients would prefer to die at home, and I would do everything humanly possible to fulfill this wish.

Do you let patients decide when they want to die, or do you keep on giving medications and helping them until the end?

I give them only as much medication as is necessary to keep them comfortable. I will help them until they die, but when they refuse to have any further dialysis or any further surgery, which may prolong their lives by a few weeks or perhaps months, I understand their wishes.

What can one say to the elderly dying cancer patient in a nursing home who is obsessed with the desire to go home? We checked it out and it is impossible for her to be at home.

I think you have to level with her and tell her honestly why it is impossible for her to go home. This is a reality that she may have to learn to face. If the reasons are questionable you may be able to help her family overcome their fears or anxieties. With a little additional help, such as visiting nurses, you may be able to convince the family to take their mother home to die. They need enough back support and someone they can call if they are in trouble.

Many patients want to die at home, or are almost forced to do so because of finances and hospital admission policies. The patients' families may also wish this. Would you please comment on how health service professionals can help these patients and families, or even help them arrive at a decision?

I'm very much in favor of allowing patients to die at home. Not for financial reasons especially, but because patients usually wish to die in their own familiar environment rather than to have their life artificially prolonged in a hospital where they can be visited only on a limited basis. If you share with a family the advantages of the last final days or weeks at home, many family members will then decide about the possibility or feasibility of such an arrangement. We have to train more homemakers and we do need more visiting nurses and physicians who make house calls before this is possible for many patients.

If a patient is beyond medical help and wants to go home to die, isn't that the same as euthanasia?

It is the same as euthanasia only if you translate the word as "a good death." It is not mercy killing. It means simply allowing the patient to die with peace and dignity in his own familiar environment, and I am proud each time I can make this possible.

Do you think we will ever permit a person to die with dignity, rather than to use gadgets to prolong life?

I think in spite of all our unhappiness with these extraordinary means and life-prolonging procedures, the majority of the world population still dies without gadgets, and it will hopefully always be so.

In view of the pending legislation on euthanasia, what are your feelings on the subject?

I find it sad that we have to have laws about matters like this. I think that we should use our human judgment, and come to grips with our own fear of death. Then we could respect patients' needs, and listen to them, and would not have a problem such as this.

A young intelligent man with a "brilliant future" ahead of him suddenly finds himself a quadriplegic. Does this man have the option to decide if he is to go on living with only his brain functioning or should he be allowed to choose to die with dignity? (That means discontinue all life-saving measures and drugs.)

I think any young man who finds himself in this predicament needs all the help he can get, to show him ways and means of still functioning as a total human being. There are many people in our chronic patient hospitals, and in our VA hospitals, who are quadriplegics. If you visited some of these patients and saw what they are able to do, you would be surprised to see that they find meaning in their lives and are productive. As long as they have their brains, as long as they can still think, and use their eyes and their ears, and communicate, they should be given all the help possible to show them that life can still be meaningful and beautiful. I would take such patients to others who have gone through such a crisis, and have found ways and means of functioning. We should not discontinue life-saving measures as long as the patient's brain is functioning. This is my personal opinion.

Who should decide how long to maintain "support systems," the patient, the family, the physician, or society? Must each case be individualized, or are there valid generalized criteria? What factors are considered, the family needs, the quality of life, or the expense?

As long as the patient can express his needs, I think we should maintain a support system, because it means that the patient is still a functioning human being. If the patient is nonfunctioning and not communicating, the family, the physician, and the interdisciplinary team have to get together and make a joint decision. Each case should be discussed on an individual basis. I don't think we have valid generalized criteria, except for the definition of death, as outlined in Henry Beecher's *Harvard Report.*

Aren't we playing God when we don't allow patients to die and we use drugs on them to keep them alive?

A child who formerly would have died from polio-myelitis, is now kept alive by giving him a prophylactic medication to prevent the illness; an old woman who formerly would have died of pneumonia is now kept alive with antibiotics. Is this playing God?

What do you say to a patient who seriously requests mercy killing from the medical staff?

I have to find out first why he cannot bear his present situation anymore. Maybe he has so much pain that he can't tolerate it; then I have to increase his pain medication. If he has been deserted by his family, I see if I can contact the family. If he is a man who needs to be in control of his life and who cannot tolerate having no control over his dying, then I give him assistance so that he can control certain procedures, maybe the choice of his food, maybe the time of his bath, or the number of visitors he can have at the hospital. He then has the feeling that he is still in control of many things. If he signs himself out of the hospital and refuses to take medication, he has the right to do so. If the patient is not mentally ill, we have to allow him this decision. If he is mentally ill, I would naturally request a psychiatric consultation, and see if we can get him into a better emotional state to make this decision rationally and in accordance with his real wishes.

When a patient has reached acceptance and the family has accepted it too, why not remove the machinery that keeps the patient "alive"? If the hospital still wants to prolong the life, what can the family do to let the patient die with dignity?

A patient's family can always ask for a consultation. They can transfer the patient to another facility, or take him home. The simplest way, perhaps, but not always a successful one, is to talk to the physician in charge, to see if he can accept the decision reached by the patient and the family.

I do not favor euthanasia in reference to incurable diseases. But at what point should physicians decide to cease prolongation of life by life-saving methods and medication? I am thinking of the financial burden inevitably placed on the family left behind; sometimes it is overwhelming.

We found some very general rules, which we use often as guidelines in making these decisions. When the patient has reached the stage of acceptance and the family is also at peace, the patient often asks to stop all life-prolonging procedures. We would respect this request under most circumstances, especially if we are sure that the patient has no chance of cure or of a remission. This naturally does not mean that we discontinue the necessary fluid intake, and that we do not give them the necessary physical care and pain medication, if these are indicated. We would also at this time discuss the possibility of a transfer home with the family, in order to allow the patient to die in a familiar environment. If the family is taught how to give injections, if we notify the visiting nurses association, and if we as physicians make occasional house calls, most families are able to handle such patients quite well.

6

Where Do We Best Care for Our Dying Patients?

A woman whose husband is dying of cancer wants him to die in the hospital so her two children will "not have to face his death." The man has made it very clear he never wants to go back to the hospital. How can I work with the wife to change her feelings about this? She will not even acknowledge his diagnosis or impending death with the children.

I do not know how old the children are, but I am a strong believer that patients should be allowed to die at home and the children should share these last few weeks or days with the father. It is important that you are not angry with this wife, who is obviously not ready for the impending death of her husband. If you really care for her, if you can spend time with her, if you can help her to express her anguish about "her husband deserting her and the children," then you may be able to help her face the reality and with some additional help of perhaps a visiting nurse and some house calls on the part of the physician, you may be able to convince this woman to help her husband to die at home.

Should we encourage dying patients to stay home with their families for their sake and for the family's sake so that the needs can be adequately met?

Yes, if the family agrees to take the patient home and if there is enough help available. Most patients would prefer to stay at home and I would certainly encourage this.

Would terminal patients be able to adjust better to impending death if they were allowed to die in their homes surrounded by the family rather than in an institution?

Most patients prefer to die at home, but there are a few who prefer to die in a hospital. Mothers, for example, who do not want to expose their children to the final crisis, or people who have been very lonely and have had poor family relationships, sometimes prefer to die in an institution. You have to evaluate each case, and if a patient prefers to die in an institution, you should not push for discharge. The majority of our patients have preferred to die at home and we make every possible arrangement to make this wish come true.

Should dying patients be segregated? By this I mean should we have special hospices or wards for dying patients?

It does not matter a great deal whether dying patients are put together on the same ward or intermixed with other patients who can get well. It is much more important how the staff feels about these patients. The general atmosphere is more important than the location of the patient. We have found special units for critically ill patients, and especially the hospice idea, extremely helpful, not so much because the patients are segregated, but because you can hand-pick a staff who is comfortable in the face of dying patients and you therefore have an environment of love, acceptance, care, and hope. Also, they eventually become specialists in terminal care, who can keep the patients physically and emotionally as well as spiritually comfortable.

Do all patients desire a specific kind of environment at the time of death? And the family?

Not all patients are conscious. Not all patients are able to express their views at the time of their dying. This is why it is so important that we all make our arrangements and express our wishes in terms of our final care when we are young and healthy. The majority of our patients would have liked to die at home. A very few patients, especially parents of young children, prefer to die in the hospital, out of a need to protect their children from a sad reality. In our opinion this deprives the children of a very important part of working through the death of a parent, thus making it more difficult to accept.

What about the patient who accepts his death and wants to go home. Is there any way he can? Even if the physician and family disagree?

No patient will be able to go home if both the physician and the family disagree. Who would take care of this patient if the family is unwilling to do that? I would join forces between clergy, nurses, and social worker and try to help the family come to grips with the impending death of their relative and offer them assistance in taking the patient home. If the patient's family is not willing to do that, the patient will be better off staying and dying in the hospital.

How can one approach and help terminal patients in an out-patient department? We have a tumor clinic and the patient knows his diagnosis.

I think a waiting room of a tumor clinic lends itself beautifully to informal get-togethers and somewhat informal group sessions. Not only is the staff available for anxious and nervous patients, but much group therapy goes on among the patients, some of whom have gone through the turmoil and are quick to help newcomers who have not yet become accustomed to the difficult waiting period in a tumor out-patient clinic. If a room adjacent to such a waiting room can be made available to relatives and patients who feel like talking about more private matters, a social worker or counselor could be of tremendous help in such an area.

What place does group therapy have with terminally ill patients and their relatives?

We have not been successful in putting terminally ill patients together in regular group therapy. You cannot talk about dying from 3:00 to 4:00 P.M. on Friday afternoon when you are terminally ill. There are days when the critically ill patient wants to talk about brighter things in life and you cannot schedule talks about dying. Also, these patients are in different stages at different times. It has not worked well in our experience. It is different when you get a group of parents of leukemic children together. Group therapy has been very effective with relatives of terminally ill patients, especially if they are trying to cope with the same critical illness.

7

The Family's Problems
After Death Has Occurred

How could you help a mother who could not bring herself to talk with her dying child, and then, in retrospect, tortures herself with what she should have done?

I think all of us who have lost someone we loved have moments when we torture ourselves and wonder if we could not have done a better job. In our society it is extremely rare to find a mother who is comfortable in talking to her dying child about the child's death. I think you have to relate this to the mother and be available to her when she wants to talk about it. If she goes through a prolonged, undue grief process with increased feelings of guilt and self-torture, she may need some professional counseling.

I have a question on how to handle a family in the case of the death of an elderly man who died after a long hospitalization for anemia. The family sits with him all night in a small country hospital; he dies at 4:30 A.M. His wife is allowed to stay for a short time until her son leads her away. The nursing staff then commences to wash and pack the body—"the normal care of the body after death" procedure. The body is wrapped in a sheet and taken to the morgue which is a small clothes closet where an emergency stretcher is kept. The wife comes back at 6:45 A.M. and wants to see the body once more. Permission is refused because of the state of the deceased. Should she be allowed this privilege? Should the body be unpacked and taken back to the room?

I think it is important to allow the family enough time to stay with their deceased relative. When the family is then ready to leave, you can ask if they plan on coming back again within a short time. Explain to them what is going to happen and give them the option of staying a little longer or, in case they change their minds, coming back a second time. They will know that the body has been packed and if it is very necessary, you may ask an orderly to unpack the body once more in order to help the family to come to grips with it. If you have a good relationship with the funeral director, you can ask him to talk to the family and invite them to come to the funeral home later on after the necessary procedures have been done there.

Should a member of a helping profession show his emotion when a patient dies?

I wonder why we should not.

At what point does grief become a pathological reaction? I am trying to help someone whose family physician told her to "snap out of it" yet she feels she needs a psychiatrist because she is so full of guilt. She got into an argument with her husband and he died sud-

denly and she is so depressed. She picks me to talk to yet I can't overrule her physician. I am only a nurse and a neighbor.

I have to refer to your last sentence before I answer your question. You say, "I'm *only* a nurse and a neighbor." I don't understand why nurses or neighbors, for that matter, have to undersell themselves. I have seen more dying patients helped by nurses than by a physician or anybody else. If it had not been for the nurses and the clergy I don't know what would have happened to my hundreds of patients. A nurse who empathizes, who obviously has some feeling for this woman, can help this woman probably better than the physician who tells her to "snap out of it" which is a silly request. If she has such unresolved guilt that she cannot just simply snap out of it, she may need professional counseling to help her out of her guilt feeling that she "killed her husband." In the meantime, you are the one who can stand by and let her ventilate and talk. You will help her much more than somebody who wants to simply "brush it under the carpet."

When a patient's family asks you, "Did he die in pain?" or "Did he say my name before he died?" do you tell the truth?

I would not tell a family member that the patient called a name when in fact he did not do it. When they ask about pain and the patient did have pain, I would say, "Yes, there was some pain but we tried our best to keep him as comfortable as possible" if this is the truth. You should not lie to family members because if you tell them phony stories they sense it and will be

more upset thinking it was probably much worse than
it was in reality.

*If the family of a cancer patient refuses to accept the
fact that their mother is dying, what can you do to
help the family after she has passed on? How can you
make it easier for them to talk about it if they still find
it difficult to talk?*

It sometimes takes months or a year until a family
can talk about it. All you have to do is to convey to
them that you are reachable and available when they
are ready to talk about it and eventually they will find
the way to you when they are ready to share their
unfinished business with a friend.

*When the stages of dying as you described in your
book,* On Death and Dying, *have not been worked
through by the family before death, how do you deal
with it after death? How can it be worked out?*

The family has to go through all the stages the second time after death.

*Should a member of the helping profession show his
emotion when a patient dies? Did you have lots of
tears at the beginning of your work?*

I still have lots of tears.

*A wife promised her husband a few days before his
death that she would be with him when he died, but
she was not with him when it happened. She now feels*

guilty and regrets the promise. How can she work through this now?

You have to sit with her and listen to her feelings of guilt and broken promises. We have all promised many of our patients that we would be with them when it happened and we spent our weekends with our family only to be informed on Monday morning that our patient had died. It is more difficult when this involves a close member of the family. I think you have to learn to convey to these people that they can only be human, not superhuman. Next time we may be more careful and say, "I will try to be with you."

Could you please elaborate more on what to do or say to the family or friend of a dying person or somebody who has already died? There seems to be a need to find a reason for the death. Why is this always necessary?

I don't think it is necessary to justify the death. We do not know the reasons in any particular case. It is very hard to find it appropriate and necessary, especially when we are faced with the death of a child or of a young person. I think this arises from our own need to rationalize and to find some meaning in the death of a loved one because we are ill-equipped and don't know what to say to a bereaved family. We try to find something special in the death in order to console the family. I feel the best consolation is to simply hold the person's hand and share your own honest feelings with that member of the family. If you do not desert the bereaved family, if you continue to visit them even after all the relatives and friends have gone, then I think you can convey some of your real feelings and will help the family through the grief process.

If the patient and family come through and accept death before it occurs, does the family go through mourning after death?

There is always some grief and mourning, but no grief work. That means no remorse, no feeling of, "Oh, God, if I had only done this or that," and no guilt.

I would like to have your thoughts on grief. Is it possible or normal to grieve for a loved husband of many years who died not long ago after a very long illness and yet not really miss him?

Yes, I think this is possible. I think a wife who has attended her husband over a long period of illness has been able to grow through the preparatory grief and is still sad about his death but doesn't necessarily have to miss him. The sense of loss is also coupled with a great sense of relief when a long illness and suffering is over.

If a child wants to visit the cemetery frequently after her father's death can anything be done to help her?

Yes, I think I would give her a lift to the cemetery and would not discourage her. I am much more concerned about relatives who avoid the cemetery, who avoid talking about their dead, than those who face the reality and go to the cemetery to work through their grief.

Is the anticipatory or preparatory grief process similar to or the same as the grief process after death when no anticipatory grief has taken place?

Yes, except the anticipatory grief has the advantage that it is still possible to talk to the terminally ill patient, to perhaps "finish unfinished business," something we cannot do after death has occurred. The postdeath grief usually is longer when no anticipatory grief has taken place prior to death, as in the case of a sudden unexpected death.

8

Funerals

Many relatives ask us about assistance in funeral arrangements especially when a death has been unexpected and the family is left in utter shock and denial, or in a stage of confusion and anger. Many patients request that their bodies be donated to medical schools or they ask for cremation, to the dismay of their families.

It is of utmost importance that we—the living and healthy—make our wishes known to our families (and lawyers) and that we all have a last will prepared before illness or death occurs. In this manner the family can calmly express their views and objections at a time when we are not emotionally upset. We all should choose a funeral home ahead of time and—if we should so desire—join a memorial society which can assist us at the time of need.

Donations of organs have to be done immediately after death occurs and the family should have the necessary information as to whom to notify in the case of sudden death, in order to gratify the wishes of the deceased.

When all this information has to be collected at the time of death it is often too time-consuming and compromise solutions result which are often disappointing and quite costly to the family.

Do you feel that the American ritual of viewing the deceased and elaborate funerals, etc., is destructive?

I think people should express their own wishes in regard to funerals. Unfortunately there are many social pressures which often require much too elaborate and expensive funerals and are really unnecessary. We have to understand that funerals are meant to gratify the needs of the family and the relatives and not the deceased. My personal belief is that the viewing of the body is only necessary if the family has not been prepared for the death of their relative, as in the case of a sudden unexpected death. In this circumstance it is important that the family can view the body before the funeral in order to face the reality of the beloved one's death. Otherwise, if there has been a prolonged illness, I regard the viewing of the body an unnecessary ritual. I also believe personally in very simple funerals with a closed casket and brief meeting with the family and relatives which gives them an opportunity to talk together about the deceased, to share memories and a meal together. I think that the elaborate expensive display of an open casket with all the makeup in the slumber room enforces the belief that the person is only asleep and in my personal opinion would only help to prolong the stage of denial.

What do you think about funerals? Do you believe they prolong agony or result in acceptance?

I believe a simple ritual is necessary to publicly and openly face the reality of the death; to be together once more and to share memories together. But the elaborate unnecessary ritual with all its commercial aspects not only prolongs the agony of the family, but adds further expensive costs to the already horrendous expenses that the family often has had to endure during a long illness.

My family and I are funeral directors. We are generally close to those we serve, and especially with children we try to take extra time to talk and listen. What counseling advice would you have for us?

Funeral directors have often misused the family's feelings of guilt and unfinished business in order to commercialize their products and to have greater profits in their business. This part of the funeral business I intensely dislike. There are funeral directors who are not exclusively commercially oriented and who truly care for the families of the people they serve. I find it very sad that we have to have such elaborate and expensive funerals which serve no purpose except, perhaps, to alleviate some guilt feelings on the part of the family. I think if funeral directors would listen to the needs of the families, also the financial needs and requests for simplicity, they could help tremendously and they would have a much better reputation. Also, funeral homes should be open for visits by young people, church groups, and high school children—to help them consider death as a part of life.

9

Family and Staff Deal
with Their Own Feelings

Do families of terminally ill patients also go through the stages of dying as the patient does, but not necessarily when the patient does?

Yes. Family members and staff usually "limp behind in the stages."

You have talked about the families of patients who are dying and helping them accept their loss, but what of those families and individuals who have not reached the stages of acceptance before the death of a loved one?

They will have to go through all the stages after death has occurred.

How do you handle death in your own family—a parent, for example—since you are so emotionally involved? Is it possible to be of help?

It is possible, but it is much more difficult when it's a member of your own family. If you feel unable to do it, you may be able to get somebody from outside the family who can talk about this with less emotion and probably be far more helpful. It is again a question of how comfortable you are. You can even reach a point where you can do it with your own mother.

Please relate ways a person can help the family serve their dying member and still respect their own needs.

It is very important that you help the family so that they are also allowed to live their own lives. That means that if a mother is dying, a young daughter or son should not be forbidden to date or go to a movie. Family members have to have their own time to re-cuperate, to recharge their batteries, especially if it is a prolonged dying process. Without this, they are going to be drained, emotionally and physically exhausted before the relative dies. It is up to you to help them in this and prevent them from feeling guilty.

Do the friends and relatives of a patient go through the five stages the same as he does?

Yes, anybody who is really involved with a termi-nally ill patient has to pass through certain adjust-ments, either prior to death or after death occurs.

How do you prepare husbands, wives, mothers, and fathers for the death of their loved ones?

You start early when the family is still well and can help each other to face the reality that all of us have to die so that it is not such a shocking experience when it happens "unexpectedly."

How would you deal with parents who gave specific orders before the admission of a young married son for a terminal illness (cancer of the lung) not to discuss his illness with him?

I would tell the parents that I'm treating an adult married man and that the contract is between the patient and myself. If they insist on "not telling him," they always have the right and the freedom to choose another physician.

(Young patients are often financially dependent on their parents long after age twenty-one, especially in the case of an extremely expensive terminal illness. This has deprived many of our young adult patients of choosing their own physicians!)

Grandmother can't talk about the death of my grandfather or his cancer and he needs to talk about it. She seems to deny it and he expresses it verbally with statements like "that stinking cancer." They seem to be always together, so how can I handle this because I see my grandfather has a great need. What can someone do to bring it out?

If Grandmother does not leave your grandfather alone, you can say in front of her, "Grandpa, you hate that cancer, don't you?" and open the conversation so he can share with you his needs to talk about it. Grandma may then leave the room if she cannot handle it, or she may ask you explicitly to stop talking about it. You may then say to her that maybe Grandpa needs to talk about it and your grandfather will help you out.

How does a nurse handle a physician who becomes totally angry when he has a critically ill patient? I'm sure his anger is a sign of his not accepting the patient's death, but what do we do with him?

Instead of getting angry back at him or instead of taking his anger personally, it might help if you'd just walk over to him one day and say, "It's tough, isn't it?" If you can empathize with his anguish, he may then open up and share with you the difficulties he encounters in facing the deaths of the patients he so desperately tries to save.

Is the anticipatory grief process similar to or the same as the grief process after death when no anticipatory grief has taken place?

There are minor differences in the anticipatory grief process. The patient really mourns impending losses and so does the family. In the grief process after death the family mourns a past loss. The latter usually takes longer. The former will take a long time only if the patient or the family is not allowed to grieve.

Do you ever cry with a patient? Half of me says, "It's okay; if it's my honest gut reaction it should be shared." The other half of me says, "Why am I crying?" Maybe I haven't worked through my own feelings enough to be working with these patients.

Yes, I have cried with my patients. Sometimes I have tears in my eyes when I sense this is my last visit with a patient I have cared for for a long time. I do not feel that it is unprofessional to have tears in your eyes. It is not a question of not having worked through enough of your own feelings; it is rather a question of how much you are willing to share your own humanness.

You gave the example of the mother of a dying child going through the various stages to the final acceptance of death. Is it typical of people close to the dying person to do this and do they experience the stages prior to, at the same time, or after the dying person?

Family members usually limp behind. Very rarely do they go through the stages before the patient goes through them. Very rarely are they all at the same stage. Most of the time the dying patient is ahead of them.

I want my contact with dying patients to relieve my own anxiety about death exclusively, and I want to use them as a tool to reach my own stage of acceptance. Comment?

If you "use" your patients for your own needs, you will not be able to help them and give them much and you will receive as little as you give.

With regard to the patient during rehabilitation after traumatic accidents or illnesses—i.e., paralysis and/or amputations—the family is lagging behind the patient in reaching acceptance and, thus, may retard the patient or prevent him from reaching the fullest potential. What are various ways to help the family reach acceptance?

When any patient is ahead in the stages of acceptance and the family lags behind, you have to spend all of your time and efforts on the family to help them work through their own anger, bargaining, and depression so that they can accept the limited functioning or, perhaps, the impending death of their relative and thus help the patient indirectly. Remember though that you should not push them, otherwise you do more harm than help.

How can we help family or others accept the death of a loved one before it occurs, i.e., when the person's still healthy, and after the death has occurred?

By loving them each day so that we have no unfinished business and no regrets when the time comes.

If you are faced with a family after death has occurred, make yourself available and assist them in going through the stages of anger, depression, and ultimately acceptance.

How do you react to relatives of the dying? Do you try to talk with them, be kind to them, what?

Relatives of dying patients are human beings just the same as dying patients. Sometimes all they need is the silent companionship of a caring human being when they do not need to talk. Sometimes they need kindness, and if you feel kind to them you share this. Sometimes they need to talk about more factual matters: *e.g.*, prognosis, different tests that the patient has to undergo, and then you talk with them about those needs. It is important to elicit the family's needs and respond to their needs and not go with the preconceived notion that your "role is to be kind."

You say be honest and share your gut reactions. I agree in the majority of instances, but does this include saying "I'm afraid of my feelings about death and

*haven't resolved them yet" to a patient? Is it better
to resolve them first and then talk to a patient?*

Anyone who can admit that he is still afraid about
his own feelings about death and has not resolved
them and is comfortable enough to say so, is not really
petrified. I have shared many of my own ambiguities
and concerns with patients and this can often help as
a vehicle to open up the patient and share his own
concerns with me. I think our fear of saying or doing
the wrong thing is exaggerated. As soon as the patient
sees that you really care and that you, too, are human
with human concerns, he will feel much more comfortable and will be much more able to share his own
feelings.

*How can we tell how we will accept our own death one
day? We answered your questionnaire.* Is this one
way to do it or is it something we don't really know
until we experience it?*

I think we can only speculate how we are going to
face it. We are never sure until it really happens, but
there is a time when you begin to be so comfortable
about it that your guess is pretty accurate.

What can we do to be less afraid of suffering?

This is a difficult question. I think one way of over-
coming your fear of suffering is to spend time with
people who are going through a crisis and help them.
Gradually you will become less afraid of it yourself.

* A questionnaire is handed to all participants in our seminars on the care of dying patients. One purpose of the questionnaire is to get students to recall their experiences of death and
to confront their own thoughts on the subject.

How does one begin the process of accepting death before it becomes imminent?

It should start in young life by visiting nursing homes, chronic disease hospitals, and terminally ill patients, by contemplating your own death, by making your last will, and by discussing such matters with your family long before you are sick. Children should be allowed to visit patients and to attend funerals. We should also take down the signs in our hospitals and nursing homes which say, "No children under age 14 are allowed to visit."

How can someone in the medical profession who is very uncomfortable about taking care of dying patients go about coping with the process of death and dying?

He has several options. I think the first step is to admit that he is uncomfortable, which you are doing by raising this question. The second one is that he should try to talk with some people in the area of thanatology to identify what specifically makes him uncomfortable. I think all of us are uncomfortable at the beginning in our career and the more time we spend with these patients, the more comfortable we become. Some counseling may shed light on the reasons for his discomfort. If it is interfering with his work, he may consider going into a specialty where he has little to do with dying patients; namely, dermatology or ophthalmology.

Regarding the fear of death, I feel it is basically fear of the unknown. You said that most people getting married are also facing the unknown; however, one can talk to other people who have married and you can ask them how it is with them. We can't do this regarding death. It is something we will never know until it happens to us. At best, it is an inadequate thing we do.

This is true, but I do not feel that the fear of death is really a fear of the unknown. People who have a very concrete concept of life after death and truly believe it are also afraid of dying and go through the same stages.

What is the best way for the person talking to the dying patient to help himself with his "dying fear" problem?

I think members of the helping profession who work with terminally ill patients should first work with patients who are not of their own age. If you expose a young student nurse to a young girl of her own age who is dying, she may become so overwhelmed that she will not be able to function. If she has had a few good experiences, perhaps with elderly people or people of an age and sex different from her own, she will see that it is not difficult and that very often the terminally ill patient helps her come to grips with her own fear of death. Gradually and slowly she should be able to work with people of her own age and sex. Nobody helps you more to come to peace with your own anxieties than the dying patient.

Can coming to grips with one's own death be accomplished by a continual getting in touch with one's feelings or is there a more structured framework one can use? I feel like I would be floundering and would like some assistance in which direction to point myself. I have little contact with dying patients to help stimulate me.

There are many ways we can come to grips with our own death. The first step is, naturally, to realize daily that our life is not to last forever. We can read literature, poetry, or contemplate death in the many ways that it presents itself to us in the form of music, drama, art. We can visit nursing homes, mental institutions, and hospitals to remind us that life is not all spring. And in groups with friends and people with whom we feel comfortable we can discuss this and form our own points of view. Religion contemplates death in a much broader sense, and anybody who is religiously inclined cannot help contemplate the meaning of life and, thus, the meaning of death. We have workshops throughout the United States on death and dying which attempt to stimulate discussion and thinking in the area of thanatology. These are open not only to professional people, but also to lay people, who will eventually have to face death.

How would you counsel a person who might live or die at any time, such as a heart victim?

The facing of our own finiteness is something that all of us should do long before we are ill and before we are faced with a potentially terminal heart attack. If we can learn to accept our finiteness when we are young, then we are prepared for death when it happens. When a patient has never contemplated his own death and then is recuperating from a coronary, it may be wise not to talk about it until he brings up the matter. You may initiate a discussion with the question, "Was it scary?"

You adeptly described the stages toward facing death in your lectures and in your book, On Death and

Dying, *and yet my question remains: How does one will to face his mortality? Is it something that evolves as we deal with sick and dying patients if we want it to? What are the final consequences of facing our mortality at both the gut level and intellectual level? Can we ever do it thoroughly until we are dying?*

There are many ways of facing our own mortality. One way is to spend time with critically ill and dying patients, to identify with them, to go with them through the stages and to reach a stage of acceptance of their deaths. I think each time we are able to do this on both an emotional and intellectual level it brings us a step closer to the acceptance of our own mortality. We have encountered other patients who have reached a stage of acceptance through years of suffering of different kinds—people who have a hard and difficult life, who have experienced losses before in their life, have gone through similar stages before so many times that they have reached the stage of acceptance long before they are even ill. A third possibility is that we start with our children early to expose them to old age homes, to hospitals, to talk about dying, to make our last will, and to prepare our family members for the possibility that any one of us can die at any time. If children are raised this way, they will accept death as part of life and will not have to go through all these stages when they face a terminal illness. People who were raised on a farm often accept birth and death as part of life, since they grew up witnessing both on the farm since their early childhood.

How can you prepare yourself for taking care of dying patients?

By visiting them, sitting with them, listening to them, and learning from them.

Can you discuss the techniques used in assisting a patient progress through the death process, or is it just being there, allowing him to progress at his own rate?

You simply help him to progress at his own rate and you can do this best if you have come to grips with your own personal fear of death.

I am a student nurse and someone expressed their fear of dying. I wish I could have helped them, but I felt so inadequate. Is this normal?

Very normal.

Does one who is caring for a dying patient need to go through the stages himself with each patient? Or does he enter the relationship at a previously attained stage?

We do not go through all the stages with every patient, only with those with whom we truly get involved. Though I feel I have reached the stage of acceptance, I often go through a brief period of anger and depression with my dying patients while they are in their respective stages.

How does the therapist's outward display of emotion affect the dying patient?

Display of emotion on the part of a therapist is like drugs. The right amount of medication at the right time can work wonders. Too much is unhealthy and too little is tragic.

What is the role of the social worker in dealing with the family and dying person?

We do not strictly differentiate between the different members of the helping professions. We do not want ministers to take care only of the religious needs or spiritual needs of our patients, the psychiatrists to take care only of the emotional needs, and the physicians to take care only of the physical needs. The social worker, in his old role, has always dealt mainly with the family and economic problems. In our interdisciplinary workshops on death and dying, we have very often exchanged roles. Whoever feels most comfortable with a given member of the family, or with a given patient, will almost automatically become that person's helper. Many times the social worker has dealt fruitfully with a dying patient because she had a meaningful and good relationship with them, and the minister has taken care of the social aspects, and sometimes the financial problems or the emotional needs of the family. A social worker is a very important and intrinsic part of our team, and together as an interdisciplinary group we should have enough resources to take care of all the needs of the dying patient and the family.

10

Other Staff Problems

Physicians, nurses, clergy, social workers, and other members of helping professions have received—until recently—very little help and training in caring for the critically or terminally ill patient. Our seminar, On Death and Dying, was initiated in 1966 and was at that time the only interdisciplinary seminar in the country training the different health professionals in the care of dying patients. It is no wonder then that hospital personnel still have many questions in regard to their specific roles. Many are afraid of "getting too involved," others are shocked that staff should spend "undue time" with dying patients when they are so needed for patients who can get well. Mostly they would like to help more but are at a loss to know what to say or what to do.

The biggest and ever-recurring problem is one of authority and communication, of confidence in each other and mutual trust. In the hierarchy of medicine it used to be the physician's exclusive role to relate a diagnosis and treatment plan to a patient. This was satisfactory as long as the doctor had an intimate relationship with his patient, often knew his family well, and had the time to sit and tell his patient what the latter needed to know. With modern medicine, urbanization, and specialization this old style of doctor-patient relationship is dying out. It is well known that patients in our large teaching hospitals are seen by dozens of physicians, residents, interns, externs, and an even larger number of nurses around the clock, often without having a personal relationship with any of them. The larger the number of "helping staff," the poorer the communication and the more difficult the decision as to who is to take care of each of the patient's varying needs.

Nurses used to spend most of their time in direct patient care. Now they are overburdened with keeping charts and doing paperwork, with checking modern, difficult equipment, and relaying information to the next shift.

It is in this increasingly sophisticated system that the patient can become less important than his electrolytes. The resident may know the patient's blood count but is unaware that his child has taken ill, and how little does anyone know about the patient's concepts of death or his religious convictions?

Staff problems will increase with the size of hospitals, with the increasing number of specialists, and with the appearance of more and more modern equipment (which makes a mechanical engineer out of a nurse). We cannot slow this trend but we can stop once in a while and ask ourselves *why* we are doing what we are doing. Are we serving the institution, the needs of a certain chief, or are we really doing it for the patient's sake?

We can also stop complaining about the people we work with and identify with their problems for a moment, thus understanding their anxieties and needs better. We all need a shoulder to cry on once in a while; we all need a "screaming room" to ventilate our feelings occasionally. If we share our needs and our feelings, frustrations and joys with each other, even a large teaching hospital may become a place for personal growth and better interdisciplinary teamwork.

How can one deal with those doctors who refuse to speak of death to their patients?

I think you have to respect the physician's decision, but what nobody can forbid you to do is to sit down with your patient and listen to him. The patient will then share with you his awareness of his own finiteness. This is true of any member of a helping profession be it the clergy, a nurse, friend, or social worker.

Why is it so hard for many physicians to deal with death in their dying patients?

One of the biggest problems is that we train our physicians during four years of medical school to cure, to treat, to prolong life. The only instruction they receive that has anything to do with death and dying is how to ask for an autopsy. It is very understandable, therefore, that "patients who die on them" are often seen as failures as the physician gets no training on how to be a good physician to patients who are not going to recover.

What do you tell a patient when there are no interns, doctors, social workers, and no clergy willing to come in the middle of the night?

I'll go there myself.

How can a hospital staff be educated to help dying patients and their families?

Every hospital should have seminars, workshops, or sessions where the problems of terminally ill patients are discussed, and where the staff can share their own feelings, frustrations, and anguish and try together as a team to come to grips with these problems.

How does the nursing personnel deal with dying patients and/or family in a small, private hospital where the primary physician assumes all responsibility for care and terminal conditions are not talked about to the family or the patient by the doctor?

Somebody on the hospital staff might take some time with the primary physician and listen to his reasons for this "total responsibility." He may not be aware that he can unload some of his burden onto the nursing staff, the hospital chaplain, or the social worker, if such members of the helping profession are willing to help those involved come to grips with a terminal illness. Have a team meeting and do not forget to invite the hospital administrator, who can be very important and who is often forgotten.

If appropriate, please address yourself to the following problem: How does the hospital staff assist the patient who daily has tests to determine the etiology of a problem? The patient has no overt signs of physical illness but the days run into weeks and the final diagnosis is "unknown etiology." Attached to the diagnosis is the statement, "need to wait and see." Would the same techniques be applied?

Any patient, in fact, any human being who goes through a crisis, whether it is loss of vision, loss of ability to walk, inability to be at home because of having to stay in a hospital waiting for the results of tests and the final diagnosis, will often go through the same stages and will at times become very angry and depressed and often bargain until the final verdict has been given. When a patient is left without knowing what he has, it is very often a question of a psychosomatic problem and this patient should have psychiatric evaluation as part of the general workup. The psychiatrist could then help the patient cope with a long hospitalization, the expensive stay, and the endless tests without any apparent results to him.

The only time I have experienced consideration of the issue of dying on the wards (as a medical student) is the verbal order of "DNR" (do not resuscitate) for a patient, but I feel this decision is made only for the benefit of the doctors and staff. What would you recommend be considered in this matter?

I think every patient in an intensive care unit should be discussed by the team, which should include the nurse, the social worker, the minister, and, naturally, the physicians involved in the case. The decision should be made as a joint decision with consideration of the patient's wishes and the wishes of the family.

What do I say to the patient who says, "You're ten minutes late with my pain medication. You were probably taking a coffee break"?

I think you can emphasize to the patient that you know how hard it must be to lie in the bed with pain waiting for the medication to come. If you have indeed been late, you can apologize and tell him that you did take a break and you are sorry. If you express your understanding for the patient's turmoil and can frankly admit your mistakes, you will have a much better relationship with your patient and he will respect your needs too, even one that includes taking a coffee break. Next time you may enjoy the coffee break more *after* giving the pain medication.

Could you please comment on possibilities for the management of the patient with no family or close friend ties and who is being bounced around from facility to facility and ward to ward in a big-city system.

I think you know my answer to that. It is a sad reality that most people who have no family members are often bounced around, but there are some hospitals where such patients are accepted and they are truly taken care of. I think in a system like ours we have to find a friend for such a patient, one who visits him no matter what facility or wards he is shipped to. You can be that one special friend.

I'm a nephrologist and a member of a team involved in the care of patients with chronic renal failure receiving hemodialysis three times weekly. For some of our patients it seems that our "helping" is as much a prolongation of dying as prolongation of living. A few patients go on what I call "denial binges" and "forget" to take the medicine or fail to maintain diet restrictions important to their medical problem. Can you comment on what seems to be a double bind for the dialysis team: to allow the person to have his feelings (as denial is serving a purpose) while feeling the need to help the person take better care of himself.

Patients on dialysis are very difficult patients in that they often pose these problems. Any patient who goes on extreme denial binges or forgets to take his medicine is a candidate for what we call "passive suicide". They are patients who deep down are ready to give up hope. They have a mental scale weighing all these efforts, restrictions and expenses, against the present quality of their life. Any patient who shows this kind of behavior should be talked with. I think the treatment team should have meetings with such a patient and reevaluate from time to time what the team is doing and what the patient is doing and try to understand your mutual behavior. Very often the dialysis team is unable to accept the limits of a patient and then overcompensates with unrealistic hope for the patient. This results in patients who have a much higher rate of passive suicide.

I would like your reaction to hospital situations in which traumatically and critically injured patients are not allowed to see their families during the time they are most seriously ill. Phone calls, cards, letters, and cassette recordings are allowed.

Phone calls, cards, letters, and cassette recordings are substitutes but will never replace the presence of the warm, caring person who can hold the hand of a patient during such a crisis. I think these restrictions are used for our own convenience. It is true that the seriously injured or burned patient is better off without visitors coming and going. But I think we should allow one next-of-kin to stay with a seriously ill patient without restrictions because it is often such loved ones who

give the critically ill the courage to keep on fighting
and who may help them ultimately "pull through." I
am against restricted visiting hours, even in an intensive care unit, when a patient is critically ill or appears
to be close to dying. The restriction of five or ten
minutes every hour are inhuman, both for the terminally ill patient and the family who has to sit in a
waiting room in agony and turmoil knowing that this
may be the last day of the patient's life.

Would you comment on the clergy's role for the dying.

We have interviewed and followed hundreds of
terminally ill patients and I do not know how this
work could have been done without the hospital chaplains. The hospital chaplain is often the only person
that the family allows to come in when they do not
want to be seen by a psychiatrist or when they are
afraid that outsiders may "talk with the patient about
dying." Very few people reject the clergy. The minister's specific role is naturally to help his patients spiritually—to pray with them, to give them the last rites,
if so desired, and to be available for any questions
concerning their religious needs. The minister should
be an intrinsic part of the team goal of total patient
care. Many times we have had patients who needed a
priest, even when they were not Catholic, or a rabbi
who was able to help a Protestant patient because "they
liked each other." We have used clergy not only in
denominational areas, but as an intrinsic part of our
interdisciplinary team approach with very good results.

*Why or how can we do away with equipment like
monitors that take you away from the person? I did
private duty on a cardiac monitor and know the pa-*

tient was the one I should have been checking. The patient died on me only three hours later.

I think we have to teach nurses how to get involved with dying patients in such a way that they are able to "switch gears" and get disengaged when they leave the intensive care unit or the cancer ward. It is impossible to care for terminally ill patients on a very personally involved level for eight or nine hours a day as nurses in intensive care units are expected to do. The only way they are able to manage this is to depersonalize and mechanize their work, and in the process it becomes dehumanized. An ideal hospital in my fantasy would have an intensive care unit where nurses work only four hours a day on this unit. This would enable them to get personally involved with their patients, while at the same time naturally, check the respirators and monitors. The rest of the day they could work in a well baby clinic or do paperwork in order to recuperate from this very involved and exhausting kind of work. It is not possible for someone to check the patient as a person for nine hours a day. We have to accept our own human limits. This is true not only for counselors to dying patients, but especially for nurses in intensive care units.

What are the professional requirements for a member of a team that does work such as you do? Do you know of any hospitals in the New York area that are interested in this approach to dying patients?

More and more people are now interested in special units for dying patients or special hospices and hospitals, such as Dr. Cecily Saunders' Hospice in London. A new setup in the process of being built is the Hospice, Inc., 183 Cold Spring Street, New Haven,

Connecticut 06511. This is another attempt to give ultimate final care to patients and is probably one of the
first hospitals modeled after the St. Christopher Hospice
in London. Such units or hospices need many kinds of
helping professions from nurses aides to the specialist
in pain relief. Any person interested in working with
terminally ill patients might be wise to contact this
new hospice.

*I am doing a Master's thesis on nursing attitudes to-
ward death. I have become increasingly concerned
with some of the suggestions that appear in the literature about things that nurses should know about the
patient in order to help him through the dying process.
For example, it is said that the staff should know what
the patient's coping mechanisms are and have been
throughout life, what his life-style has been, etc. It
would seem that one has this kind of knowledge in
depth only about his own immediate family, people
known over a long period of time. Do students and
staff become discouraged when they are expected to
know this information about a patient? What contribution can nonprofessionals such as nurses aides make
to conferences about a dying patient and are they
effective instruments in helping the patient through the
dying process?*

It is a mistake to think that you have to be a psy-
choanalyst or a psychiatrist to help a dying patient. It
is not necessary to know a patient's whole life history
and background as well as his coping mechanisms in
order to help him. In fact, we have seen that we are
usually better equipped to help a dying patient if we
do not read his chart and when we have little information about this person. It is our hope that we can train

human beings to *listen*. If you listen to the patient, the patient will ask you questions that are relevant at the moment. It is not even necessary to know whether a patient has been informed about his critical illness. Many times this is written in the chart and a member of the helping profession enters the patient's room with the idea that "he can talk about it." It is important to listen to the patient and to answer his questions honestly and openly. It is much more important how you personally feel in relation to death and dying. Perhaps the best example of this is a black cleaning woman, whom I observed several years ago when I was in the process of starting the seminar on death and dying. Many times when this woman entered the room of a dying patient, apparently something positive happened. One day I cornered her and asked, "What are you doing with these dying patients?" She became very defensive and emphasized that she only cleaned the room. After weeks of trying to get to know each other we finally had a cup of coffee together and she opened up with a traumatic story of a very pathetic life of suffering in a ghetto. I was about to ask her why she was telling me all this, when she told me how she once sat for hours in a hospital with her three-year-old child on her lap, waiting for a physician to come. Her little boy died in the waiting room. She ended her story with the following statement: "You know, death is not a stranger to me any more. He's like an old acquaintance and I'm not afraid of him. Once in a while when I walk into the room of some of these dying patients they look so scared that I cannot help but walk over to them and touch them and say, it's not so terrible." Because of her own acceptance of death she was able to comfort my patients by conveying her own feelings of peace to them.

I am an R.N. I was sitting holding the hand of a dying man (just letting him know I cared, shared, and was there). My functional head nurse told me to get off my duff and back to work. Help!

You are not the one who needs help. Your head nurse is the one who needs assistance.

How do you help a nursing staff deal with a situation they describe as this: The doctor is adamant that the patient not know his condition—that he has a serious disease, i.e., cancer, and that it is terminal. They, therefore, wish to avoid the patient for fear the patient will ask them questions regarding his condition.

This is a question that regularly comes up in every workshop and seminar on dying patients. The physician may know the patient well and he may be one of those few exceptional patients who needs denial to the very end. In this case it is better not to tell him that he is terminally ill. However, the patient will know, sooner or later, that he has a serious illness, and if the physician is not able to relate to him, he will then ask a minister or the nurse more detailed questions. What nobody can forbid you to do is to listen to your patients and to answer them honestly. If they ask you if they have cancer, you can refer this to the physician, who is the only one who should answer questions in terms of diagnosis. If the patient shares with you his awareness that he is not getting better or that he has more and more pain, the nurse should sit with him and share her feelings of empathy and attempt to comfort him as much as possible. Patients will very quickly sense which one of the nurses is able to sit with him and not avoid him. The patient will then tell the nurse how much he knows and will ask all the relevant questions that the nurse is able to answer. As a nurse you can frankly say, "Only your doctor can give you the diagnosis, but what I am allowed to do is to listen to you. What's the problem?" In no time he will describe to *you* his turmoil and you can help him.

Nurses are caught in a triple bind, owing alliance to doctor, hospital, and patient. What is a nurse to do in the face of a doctor's specific orders not to tell the patient his diagnosis or talk about death and prognosis when the patient gives clear indication that such discussion is desired? What is the nurse's legal responsibility and ethical responsibility?

As outlined in several questions preceding, the nurse should not be the one to give the patient the diagnosis. A physician may fire her or it may make for very difficult teamwork if the nurse steps out of her role. A nurse has many avenues to help the patient. She can ask the chaplain to visit the patient, who may then share his awareness with the minister. The patient may also share it with a nurse if she does not avoid the issue. The best, but most difficult approach, is to talk directly to a physician who seems to have difficulties and share with him her own feelings and her wish to relate more frankly to the patient.

There are usually two factions of nurses on the staff— those who believe in your concepts and those who don't. What do we do with them?

I can answer this question best by stating that there are people who believe in a life after death and others who don't. Do not try to convert the ones who don't. I think by your own comfort and contentment you will be more able to convey to others that your concepts

are helpful, not only in working with dying patients,
but in everyday living. Nurses who do not believe that
you should be open and honest with dying patients
will soon sense that you have a good relationship with
patients. They will see that you are not depressed and
morbid and exhausted at the end of the day, but you
have some very gratifying moments with dying patients where you feel you can truly help them in spite
of their "dying on you." Maybe eventually they will see
the difference and you will have more nurses on your
side.

*How do lay persons (who are able and wanted by a
dying patient) get past the secret society tactics of both
physicians and nurses to give comfort and support?
This is very hard sometimes. Physicians and nurses
often don't want outsiders lest they give away what the
patient already knows but won't share with doctors or
nurses.*

You can become an official volunteer in a hospital,
and if you are doing a good job, the staff will very
soon sense the difference you make. They will be
happy if you attend to some of their dying patients,
those who need a bit more time. Somebody who can
sit quietly and silently with them and is not called
away by the page system or other duties is appreciated
by most, envied by others, and always resented by a few.

*If a nurse on a floor with a dying patient finds the
staff, both physicians and nurses, avoiding the patient
what would be a good course of action if a conference
seems to achieve nothing?*

You can always take a few minutes before or after
your own work to come and visit the dying patient.

They require very little time and if they can have one human being who drops in on them and does not desert them, they can be helped.

How does a person in a helping profession get the physician to level with either the patient or the social worker so that someone can at least try to help the patient?

Try to start a conference or seminar on your floor with different members of the helping professions and discuss your mutual difficulties with terminally ill patients.

My experience has been that physicians, especially internists, treating terminal patients are insensitive and ill-equipped (both in training and time-wise) to deal with the problems of death and terminal illness. What are your ideas on how this situation could be remedied, especially at the out-patient level—for example, chemotherapy patients, parents of leukemic children?

The first thing we have to do is to include courses in medical schools in the art of medicine, so that more physicians become better equipped and more comfortable in dealing with terminally ill patients. The second thing we can do is to have a "screaming room" in the out-patient clinic where people who come in regularly and need to ventilate their feelings or their fears can sit with a member of a helping profession or a trained volunteer and share some of their needs. The third possibility is that every out-patient clinic can start group therapy for patients who come in regularly and also for parents of leukemic children. This has been found to be extremely therapeutic for all participants.

In our hospital we have a specialized oncology unit. Do you have suggestions as to how the staff can be helped to deal with almost continuous emotional drain? The staff tends to withdraw from emotional involvement after a time.

It is very important that cancer units and oncology services have a little room where staff can get together and share their gut reactions, needs, anxieties, and turmoils with each other. Without such sessions where "their own batteries can be recharged," the staff will be much too drained and has no other choice but to withdraw or to depersonalize and mechanize the patient care.

Should the nurse be more involved in knowing what the doctor has told the patient about his diagnosis?

Most nurses feel that it is essential to know what the patient has been told. We are of the impression that it is not very important what the physician has told the patient. What is much more important is how a patient has been told. This has never been written in any chart and no nurse will ever find this out from the physician unless she was present when this happened. A physician who is comfortable with dying patients will relate to a patient early in his illness that he is seriously ill and will then answer all the questions as they are brought up by the patient. Those patients do excellently as long as they are given hope. If a nurse who works with a terminally ill patient is not sure what the patient has been told, she simply has to listen to him. The patient will share with the nurse what he wants to talk about. He will also relate to her how much he knows. It is important for nurses to understand that this need changes from day to day, and from person to person.

How can nurses better understand and work with a physician who continuously uses extraordinary measures?

In cases like this I think it is important that inter-disciplinary seminars are started so that the other members of the helping profession can point out the problem to the physician and at least express their ambivalent feelings about such measures.

What is your initial approach? How can a nurse get a patient to talk about dying? It seems impossible to be able to walk into a room and just start talking about dying. Also, there is a problem with many physicians who don't want patients to be told (usually by request of the family), and if a nurse even intimates that death is near she stands a good chance of losing her job.

You are right. A patient should not be told about his imminent death. You do not talk with patients about dying or tell them they are terminally ill. I would find this very untherapeutic and not helpful. The meaning of "talking about death" is related to your own ability to accept the fact that a certain patient is most likely beyond medical help. When the patient faces this reality and asks you a question, it is up to you to sit down and talk with him about it. If you are uncomfortable, you will deny it and change the topic of the conversation and will not be able to help the patient. Our initial approach is usually to visit our patients, sit down and ask if they feel like talking at all. If they say yes, we then ask them what it feels like to be very sick. Very quickly the patient will ventilate his dismay about the restricted diet, the increasing pain, the avoidance of the staff, and other problems, and within two to five minutes will talk about what it's like to be a lonely, miserable, isolated, terminally ill patient. Sometimes we go into a patient's room and we ask a patient how sick he is. One patient looked in my eyes and, surprised, asked, "Do you really want to know?" When I said yes, he said, "I'm full of cancer." Within a couple of minutes we talked about what it is like to be terminally ill of cancer. Another possibility is that you simply sit down and say, "Do you feel like talking about it?" The patient will then talk about whatever is on his mind. If you are comfortable, he will approach the subject of his final care. Another good opening statement is "It's tough, isn't it?"

As a nurse I have been involved many times with the dying. If one establishes a relationship with a patient does that not mean a commitment to him? What happens when you know he needs you, but work circumstances prevent you from spending any time with him? Is this failing the patient? It is very important for me to know whether such a patient will understand.

You have to read Anselm L. Strauss and Barney G. Glaser's book *Anguish* to understand how often we avoid the patient with the rationalization that work circumstances prevent us from spending any time with him. Most of the time this is an excuse and a reflection of our discomfort in the face of a dying patient. If you have a good relationship with a terminally ill patient and you are transferred to another floor, it only takes two minutes of your time before going home to drop in on him and say hello. Dying patients understand your responsibilities to your job, they understand that people are transferred to other services, and they will forgive you for that as long as you keep in touch with them, sometimes with a postcard if you are away from the premises, sometimes, perhaps, with a phone call that takes only two minutes, or, most preferred, naturally, with a personal brief visit, which does not have to exceed five minutes.

What can you do as a therapist when the doctor chooses not to tell a patient he is dying? As an occupational therapist, I am frequently asked to give psychological support to patients. They frequently want to talk about death. I feel that I cannot help them, that my hands are tied behind my back.

Your hands are not tied behind your back. If you are explicitly asked to give psychological support to a patient that means that you have to feel comfortable to sit down with them and even talk about death if the patient approaches the subject. You can talk with a patient about anything as long as the patient initiates the conversation and as long as you do not just go into a patient's room and say, "What is it like to be dying?" when the patient is perhaps in the stage of denial. Nobody can forbid you to listen and to respond to your patients. Remember that.

Perhaps our greatest fear as chaplains, nurses, etc., is not trusting ourselves in this tension that we feel when trying to help a patient who is searching for some response. We would like to share some gut level responses, but we are afraid we may break in our controls and fail to provide any stability which is expected of us. Hence, it is easier to keep our responses at the objective clinical level.

It may be easier for you to keep your responses at the objective clinical level, but it is more helpful for the patient if you come into his room first as a human being, and then in your professional role. Because you are a human being, because you have feelings and gut reactions, you can share these with your patients and your patients will be grateful. If you come in only as a professional person, you will never be able to truly help the patient until you can also share your feelings of grief, sorrow, anguish, and sometimes pain.

We have a teen-age male patient with myocarditis, a candidate for a heart transplant. He's totally unprepared. If the parents and attending physician of such a patient do not wish the nursing staff to discuss his illness with the patient, how do you handle the situation?

You have to respect the orders of the physician and the parents, but you can express your care, your love, and your understanding to this young patient, and when you are alone in his room, he will hold your hand and ask his questions about the future operation. You can then ask the physician if you can be present during his next rounds and encourage the patient to raise the questions in your presence to the physician.

It is often difficult to make the doctor see what we are trying to do for the dying patient. Is medical education doing something about it?

Yes, there are many more medical schools now that have included the care of the dying patient in their curriculum.

You are trained to pick up a lot of these patients' cues, and this is your work, but how can a nurse or any

other staff member who is very busy on a ward and
involved with living patients better handle the situation of a dying patient on the ward? How do we get
the time unless we stay after work?*

I think your problem is that you regard dying
patients as not living patients anymore. I think a
patient who is in the process of dying is living as much
as any other patient, if not more, and needs your care,
your time, and your attention as much, if not more,
as those who are getting well and will be able to
return home. Working with, listening to, and picking up
cues from dying patients does not take any more time
than doing the same thing for patients who are better off.
It takes five minutes (and sometimes saves an hour of
anguish, discussion, and agony later on) to give that
extra care to terminally ill patient. What the staff
often forgets is that the dying patient has very few
demands. He needs to be comfortable, as pain-free as
humanly possible, and he does not demand much
except to have one human being who does not desert
him. If a nurse can stop in for a minute and ask, "Is
it tough today?" the patient will share with you what
the special problem is today and you can try to alleviate this agony. It takes very little time, and done in
the right manner will save you many hours later on.

*How do you feel about the doctor's decision as to
whether the patient should be told if his disease is
terminal?*

Patients should not be told that their illness is terminal or that they are dying. A patient should be informed
that he is seriously ill but that everything possible will be
done to keep him comfortable and to help him. When
the patient becomes "beyond medical help," he will ask

the doctor if he has any chance. If the physician levels with the patient and gives him an appropriate idea of his expectations without leaving him without hope, the patient will then be able to come to grips with it much better than if he is told that he is going to get well.

How does one assist the young doctor resident to face the fact that a patient is dying?

Young physicians are much more amenable to this kind of training than older physicians, who have been already "molded." When we try to teach the art of medicine and the care of the dying patient to medical students, we have a very high success rate. When we try to reach externs we are more successful than with interns, and after about two years of residency, it becomes almost hopeless. It is essential, therefore, to reach the medical students early in order to have better future relationships between nurses, clergy, and physicians in the care of the terminally ill patient, and to teach them the science and the art of medicine simultaneously.

Do you have any structured ways (such as groups) of helping staff to deal with their own and their patients' feelings?

Our seminars on death and dying not only dealt with the needs of the dying patient, but each seminar and patient interview was followed by a group discussion among the staff on an interdisciplinary level to share gut reactions and feelings in relation to the patients discussed. This not only helped the staff ask their questions and share their feelings, but it helped us to understand each other's problems. The nurses began to respect the physicians' difficulties more and vice versa. This has to be done in the absence of the patient and is always kept strictly confidential.

Have you had any success in lessening the resistance of the medical-surgical community to providing the means and situations where the terminally or critically ill patient can deal with the problems of his illness and possible death so present to him and his family? If so, how?

We have had hundreds of workshops, seminars, and in-depth meetings with different members of the helping professions from high school level to medical schools, and the attendance has ranged from approximately twenty-five participants up to four thousand, a slowly increasing number of whom were physicians. I think the atmosphere is changing now and there is hope that in the future our dying patients will not be so bitterly deserted.

What about restricting the visiting time in an intensive care unit to five minutes an hour when the patient will be dying within hours and then the patient dies alone—isn't this terribly inflexible?

Yes, these rules should be changed. When a patient appears to be beyond medical help, all restrictions should be lifted and at least one relative should be allowed to stay with the dying patient during this final period and not be sent out of the room at the moment of his dying. The patient should in fact be taken out of the intensive treatment unit.

What can a nurse do when a cancer patient asks, following an operation, if the cancer has spread? How

*do you hide your own reactions when you know the
doctor has not fully informed the patient?*

I think it should be up to you to inform the physician that the patient has asked directly.

*I am a physical therapist and wonder if you see the
benefit of range-of-motion exercises to help keep the
patient from feeling stiff. Also, it may be helpful to
see a new person and talk with her, to maintain circu-
lation, and hopefully make the patient more comfortable. If you don't, please state why and what you feel
is more beneficial.*

For a patient who has had a severe stroke and is
paralyzed or for a terminally ill patient who has difficulties moving around and becomes more and more
stiff, it can be a great comfort to see that a physical
therapist visits her regularly and helps her with her
range of motions, brings some sunshine to her bed,
and cares for her well-being and comfort, even if this
may be regarded as a waste of time of especially
trained staff. Any human care that can be given to a
dying patient and that helps to make him more comfortable is beneficial beyond a shadow of a doubt, and
is never a waste.

*What can you do when a patient accepts his death and
is prepared for it, when his family and the nursing
staff accepts the same, but his physician says, "No, he
will get better," or the physician keeps the patient alive
for many days, even though the family requests
otherwise?*

The family has the responsibility of signing a request sheet that will prevent the physician from using

extraordinary means and from keeping the patient "alive" against the patient's wishes and the family's wishes. The family can also make arrangements to take the patient out of the hospital or ask for a consultation by another physician who has fewer problems with dying patients. The nurse can convey her own feelings to the physician and to the family and offer alternatives.

As a chaplain who must break the news of a sudden death, how can I best help the family to accept the death?

You cannot help a family to accept death at the moment when you give the bad news. All you can do is stay with the family, allow them to cry on your shoulder, to question God, and, if necessary, be angry at God or the hospital staff without your trying to put the brakes on and without discouraging them from using angry and not always comfortable language. If you remain available to this family, not only at the moment of the bad news, but during the following weeks and months, dropping in occasionally or giving them a call, you will best help them to slowly and gradually come to grips with a sudden death. The families of sudden death victims will have to go through the same stages that the dying patients go through. They will first be in the stage of shock and denial, followed very often by tremendous anger, at those who have caused the accident, at the ambulance driver, or perhaps at the emergency room staff for not keeping the patient alive. Then they will go through a brief period of bargaining and a prolonged stage of depression, and, hopefully, ultimate acceptance.

When should the hospital staff call a minister or a chaplain?

Members of the clergy should hopefully become an intrinsic part of the treatment team in any hospital. Many patients appreciate a visit from a member of the clergy from time to time, not necessarily for any rituals or prayers, but just to get to know them so that when the patient is in need of spiritual help, he is already a friend. The patient who does not want to see a minister or chaplain should naturally not be forced, but if any patient feels lonely or is depressed, it would be very appropriate to offer him the service of the chaplain who can be a tremendous help, to the patient, the family, and to the staff. Clergy should become involved upon admission and not only when the patient is "beyond medical help."

Do you think that the total commitment a counselor must make (i.e., availability at any and all times) is too much, too great an expectation of the counselor?

Yes, it is too much. None of us can be available at any and all times, but I think you can give your telephone number to some special patients and you can tell them that if they are in a real problem situation that they can try to reach you. This is not a commitment that "whatever you do you will drop everything" and visit them, but an offer for help within your limits. This is one of many reasons for having a team, so that you can be replaced and can maintain a private life, which is mandatory when you do this kind of demanding work.

11

Old Age

Many people believe that death is a welcome friend to most elderly people. This is only partially true. Old age is not synonymous with being "glad to die." Many of these old patients who welcome death may not be in a stage of acceptance, but rather one of resignation, when life is no longer meaningful.

Our old age homes are a sad reflection of our lack of appreciation of our elders. We give them shelter, room and board, at times even color television and swimming pools, golf courses, and dancing facilities, but we deprive them of the chance to still serve, give and offer their unique services—namely, all the wisdom and experiences they have accumulated over many decades. Living means to give and to take, to receive and to serve others—and it is the latter that is often missing in our retirement centers, which results in the old man's (or woman's) wish to die, because life is not worth living anymore.

Many older people say they want to die. I don't blame them, but can you really say that you would feel the same way?

Naturally you can say that. Patients respond to you in a much more open fashion if you are honest with them. If you feel that their quality of life is really not worthwhile anymore and they express it verbally, naturally you can agree with them, but you have to add at the same time, "Is there anything I can do for you that makes life a little bit more bearable and a little bit more meaningful?" They will come up with some marvelous ideas sometimes, things that are not time-consuming but require an open, honest question and a caring human being to respond.

How do you deal with elderly people who express the wish to die, but whose death is not apparently imminent?

You have to find out what makes their lives miserable or not worthwhile and try to gratify their needs if it is humanly possible.

Do you think some of your teaching films should be shown to patients in geriatric centers?

All of the films we made on death and dying can be shown in geriatric centers as long as the patients are told what the film is all about and that they can choose to attend or stay in their rooms.

How do I help a member of my family in a nursing home reach acceptance instead of resignation? How do family members help?

The best way would be to take them home to live. It is much easier to accept one's finiteness in a familiar environment than in a nursing home where he is visited maybe once a week or once every two weeks. If this is not physically possible you should talk with the older person and explain why it is not possible for him to go home. Ask simply and straightforwardly, "What can I do to make your life truly meaningful in spite of the fact that you are in a nursing home?"

Is it appropriate to discuss their fears about death and dying with older people who keep saying they wish they were dead, but who are not ill with anything special or terminal except senility?

We should do it before they are senile.

How do you communicate with the very senile terminal patient?

Through touch, love, and excellent nursing care.

How does one deal with one's fears of the death of parents who are getting older although they are not ill or in immediate danger of dying? Does it indicate a fear of being alone?

I think it indicates that you are afraid to lose your parents. Sit with them, talk with them about it, make arrangements now before it happens, and discuss with each other what has had meaning in your life and what will make such a separation more bearable. You should do this before illness comes or before your parents have a stroke and may not be able to talk about it.

What do you say to a patient who is very old and infirm who says, "I wish I could die" or "I want to die"?

I say that I can very well understand that, and sit down and have him talk about what makes it especially difficult in his circumstance. He may say that he is terribly lonely and nobody cares if he lives. Then I'd try to convey to him that there are people who care and see if I could stimulate some people to visit this old person, to give him a feeling that he is still an important part of society. If his problem is physical discomfort and pain, I'd see that this was taken care of. If it is some financial problem that keeps him worried, I can ask for the help of the social worker. If the problem is simply that he has the feeling of having lived his life, having been satisfied with it, and feeling that it has lasted long enough and if it would last any longer it would become meaningless, then I agree with him that I would feel the same way.

I have just started working with senior citizens and it seems as if they go through the stages even though they may not have a diagnosed illness. Is that a correct observation?

This is very true, especially if they have been moved to a nursing home. They are going through the same stages that anybody will go through, not only if they face death, but if they have to come to grips with any loss. An old person who has lived at home for a long time and then is transferred to a nursing home will have to go through the same adjustments because of the loss of a home or of a family, or simply of a functioning existence.

I have an elderly lady who is eighty-five years old and who is dying. However, the daughter is always there and will not let us talk about the patient's dying. The daughter talks about how much her mother is needed and all the work there is for the old lady to do. Would you suggest that I see the patient alone?

Yes. Not necessarily to talk with her about dying, but with you she may be able to say that it is very hard to let go, that her daughter is unable to let go, that she feels guilty when she can no longer gratify the daughter's needs. You have to play it by ear and see what your eighty-five-year-old lady wants to talk about and not what you want to talk about. Someone also has to help the daughter face it.

Do you find elderly persons who face nursing homes after hospitalization willing to talk about death? I found often that they talk about "death of an active home life."

This is very true. There are many forms of death. If a patient is hospitalized and hopes to return to her home environment and instead is transferred to a nursing home, she very often talks about this and implies that "this will be my death." This is sometimes referred to as "social death."

My question concerns care in units of extended care. The patient can hear, is old, and has had many years of slow deterioration. She can open her mouth for food and is cleaned twice a week internally. How may one relieve her fear and anxiety so that she will let herself pass over?

I don't think I am able to answer this question because I don't know how she expresses her fears and anxieties. Maybe she is quite content and well taken care of and you are doing everything you can. If in her facial expressions she expresses any fears and anxieties, sit with her, hold her hand and talk with her about what might be her fear. Give her a signal that she can press your hand if she agrees and that she has another signal for the answer no and she may be able to have a meaningful dialogue with you in spite of her deterioration and apparent inability to speak.

Please comment about how to handle death with an elderly and confused person.

With an elderly confused person it is very hard to have a meaningful dialogue. I think the most important thing you can do for those patients is to give them good physical, emotional, and spiritual care. Also, reorient them each time when they cannot recognize who you are.* To talk about their concept of death or their unfinished business is too late when they are confused.

I have seen elderly patients judged incompetent and called suicidal because they refused surgery, saying they were old and ready to die. Could you comment on what you see as the rights of the patient in these circumstances and the basis of the decision of the psychiatrist.

---

* Example: "Here comes Sister Mary again. Isn't it a lovely September morning today. We will have a nice Sunday breakfast."

If a patient is very old and is ready to die and does not want to undergo any additional surgery my inclination is to accept the decision of the patient. If he is pathologically depressed, I would regard it my duty as a psychiatrist to get him out of the depression and ask him once more; if he still refuses he naturally has the right to do so. It is his life and his body.

Can you discuss death and dying in the geriatric unit? The patient often says, "I have lived long enough." How do you answer this?

I would say, "Yes, you may have lived long enough but since you are still living is there anything that we can do to make it more worthwhile so that you can truly live until you die?"

How do you help nursing home residents cope with what they miss—all that home symbolizes?

You try to make the nursing home as much a home as humanly possible and that means that you include children, not only for visiting, but for residing there at least during the day (in day-care centers) so that the old people can help with the little ones. The elderly can perhaps plant a little garden and do some woodwork and all the other things that used to make life meaningful at home.

What other ways can we make old people in nursing homes feel wanted other than day-care centers on the premises?

I think we could take them to schools—classes and seminars—where they can talk about their homes and

early life experiences in the old country, for example.
We could ask them what hobbies and interests they have.
They could have classes in woodworking for young
boys, where they could be big brothers to boys who
don't have fathers or grandfathers. There are many
assets and a lot of wisdom buried in nursing homes
that are never used and mobilized. If you would take
a little effort and find out what strengths, talents, and
assets these old people have there would be many, many
places where these assets could be used, and it would
make old people feel wanted, needed, and loved and
still of some service.

*Please discuss resignation in old people. How do I
work with these people in nursing homes?*

When somebody is old and feels unwanted and of
no earthly use anymore, he is usually in the stage of
resignation. He really doesn't want to live anymore
because life is no longer meaningful and seems to have
no purpose. As a visiting clergyman, you could talk
with them about the meaning of life, not necessarily in
theological terms, but find out what had meaning in
their younger years. Find out if any of these things can
be reapplied in old age and you can help them move
from resignation to a happier acceptance.

*How do you handle resistance and avoidance by some
people when they are faced with the infirm aged, or
with ill children?*

Those people have a problem and they may be
better off doing some other work, not working with
sick children or in a nursing home. Maybe they should

do clerical work or something that doesn't involve needy people. If you have the time and the interest in working with these people, you can find out where their resistance comes from. It may be that they had some traumatic life experience and are too afraid to get close to these people.

Length and quality of life seems to be directly related to the satisfaction of human needs: security, self-respect, self-esteem, etc. In view of this I would be interested in hearing your feelings about mandatory retirement at age sixty-five. Doesn't this relate directly to deterioration of both physical and mental health?

There are innumerable people far over the age of sixty-five who would be much better off if they could continue their routine life-style and their routine work. I am not in favor of mandatory retirement in general if I look at it purely in terms of the patient's needs. Since we do have many younger people who have to support families and have difficulties getting jobs, we would have problems without a mandatory retirement. I presume that the trend will be that the age of the mandatory retirement will go further down rather than up. I think we can teach our young people in their thirties and forties to prepare themselves for a meaningful retirement so that this will no longer be related to deterioration of physical and mental health. If we prepare our lives in such a manner that we develop enough broad interests, hobbies, and enough internal resources, to be able to stand on our own, emotionally, physically, and financially, then I think retirement does not have to be the beginning of rapid deterioration. Every human being should develop some hobbies and interests which are not related to his work and his income, which he could then continue with enjoyment after his retirement.

Thinking of quality of life, what do you think of superb nursing care for the senile? Nurses are so proud of keeping these old people alive!

They should be. I have very rarely, however, seen superb nursing homes. Even a senile human being is entitled to dignity and tender loving care.

What are the alternatives for the chronically ill or elderly—nursing homes, hospitals, foster homes? Which of these do you believe has the most positive value?

I think the best would be if their own family could take care of these patients. If they are no longer able to take care of their parents or grandparents then I think foster homes or small nursing homes which offer very much of a family home environment would probably be the best choice.

How would you answer an eighty-six-year-old grand-mother when she states, "I wish I would die" or "I want to jump off the bridge." She is in restraints in a nursing home.

If I were in restraints in a nursing home at age eighty-six, I would also jump off a bridge if I had the energy to do so. Has anybody ever tried taking her off the restraints, putting her in a wheel chair, and taking her for a walk in the garden? These little serv-ices to old people can make their lives, if not pleasant, then at least a bit more bearable.

How does one help an aged parent accept the death of a middle-aged child?

Any parent who loses a child goes through a tremendous loss and it will take years, sometimes, to come to grips with the loss of a child. It does not matter if the child is five years old or fifty years old. For the parent, he will always remain a child. You continue to visit those parents, you let them talk about it, you let them show you pictures of the deceased child, and find out how best you can help them. Needs differ from parent to parent.

What are the implications for care of the aged and aging from your work with the dying? Is collective or communal living the answer? Senior citizens—are they the best possibility?

I don't like communal living and senior centers which are exclusively for old people. This, to me, is a tremendous segregation of old people and is not really what life is all about. I think old people do much better if there are different generations around, and especially children. There will always be old people who can't stand children, but they were not able to stand children even when they were young. Those people can go into an area where children are excluded, but for most average people to have a little laughter, to see some children coming home from school, to see children in a park or on a swingset, will give them distraction and pleasurable memories and someone to talk to, and children love to listen to stories of old people.

When an eighty-two-year-old man asks if he is dying, what does one answer? He is at home but the doctor is out of town. The patient looks weak and tired but exhibits no really critical symptoms.

I let him talk about his feeling that he is dying; he may be right. You don't always have to have a disease that terminates your life. Eighty-two-year-old people usually know when they are close to death. This reminds me very much of old Eskimos who simply get up from the dinner table one evening, look around at each member of the family, and then slowly walk out to die during the night. People, especially old people, know when their time is close and they are usually right.

Have you interviewed very old people in a nursing home who feel rejected by their families?

I have talked to innumerable people, medium old and very old, in nursing homes, many of whom have been rejected by their families, and they feel very miserable and lonely. Those are the people we try to visit in order to give them a little bit of a feeling that somebody still cares.

How would you hear or interpret the statement: "When I get too old to live, I'll go out in the woods and take a shotgun with me"?

I don't think this requires much interpretation. What this person is saying is that he does not want to get too old so that he is a burden and end up in a nursing home, usually rejected by the family, in a meaningless existence. These people want to be able to "call their last shots."

12

Questions of Humor and Fear, Faith and Hope

Could you comment on the humor you find dying patients exhibit? I do not mean a cynical humor but the kind that reflects a healthy attitude to life and living. I see having a sense of humor as a healthy sign and a good teaching mode.

I have very much enjoyed the humor of my dying patients. I can laugh very heartily with some of my patients. They have a tremendous sense of humor once their unfinished business has been taken care of and if you do not enter their rooms with a long, grim face, finding it somewhat perverted to laugh with a dying patient. People who have exhibited a good sense of humor during their lifetime will naturally maintain their sense of humor in their dying.

My husband was scheduled for lung surgery two months ago. He suddenly became very fearful. I asked the head nurse at 7:30 A.M., half an hour before surgery, "If he should start to die and there's no help

*for him, will you let me go into surgery for a few min-
utes." She refused. At 7:35 A.M. they discovered that
he had hepatitis and would have died on the operating
room table. My instincts were right. He is now afraid
to return and the family is torn as to what to do. What
can we do?*

Discuss this with your family physician or with the
physician on the treatment team for whom you have
the most trust and feel most comfortable with and let
him give you the options. He will then be able to talk to
your husband about it and he's ultimately the one who
has to agree or disagree to the next steps.

*You say, "It is basic knowledge that in our uncon-
scious, death is never possible in regard to ourselves.
It is inconceivable for our unconscious to imagine an
actual ending of our life here on earth." Mother
Nature seems to equip living things according to their
needs. Could it perhaps be that the subconscious is
not equipped with this concept because there is no
such thing as death of the psyche? Would this not be a
possible indication from Man's own science of the
reality of religious truths concerning life after death?*

I believe that the soul or the spirit continues to live
and it is conceivable that this is the reason why it is so
difficult for us to conceive of our own death.

*If you prepare a person to accept death, aren't you
making death more of a certainty than it possibly is
(medically speaking)? Perhaps if the patient were able to
keep on struggling he would recover. Miracles do
happen.*

Oh yes, miracles do happen, but I have never seen the miracle of a human being able to prevent his death ultimately. All of us have to die and the sooner we accept the reality of our own death the sooner we can truly start living. Many patients who were able to overcome their fear of death and faced their own finiteness were then able to use all their internal energy and resources in the fight to get well and to get home.

Do you feel patients describe death as catastrophic because it is beyond their control and understanding?

For some people the greatest fear is that it is beyond their control and beyond their understanding, but the real fear which is repressed and unconscious, is because of a view of death as a catastrophic destructive force and has ultimately to do with our own potential destructiveness. I believe if we could come to grips with our own destructiveness, we would then be able to overcome our own fear of death.

A nurse raised the following question following an interview with a dying patient in front of an audience: "To me, death is a very personal experience. I have lost four close friends. Isn't this interview a bit dehumanizing? My gut reaction is we are in a zoo looking at this person dying even though it is a learning experience." What is your reaction?

When I do interviews in front of an audience, I have mixed feelings about it just as you have. I feel, however, that the patient would not volunteer for such an interview if he did not expect to get some benefit out of it. All of our patients have been asked if they would voluntarily come for such interviews. Many of them have responded favorably. I think one reason terminally ill patients are grateful for this kind of dialogue is that this is a period of their life when they feel that they are a burden, useless, and "no good for anything." If we then ask them if they will do us a service they feel, often for the first time in weeks or months, that they can contribute something, even if it is nothing but shedding some light into the mysteries of dying and helping us to be of better assistance to other patients. For this reason I still continue interviews. I do not find it dehumanizing. I think if you sense how close and how caring and loving some of these interviews become you cannot possibly put the label "dehumanizing" on them.

What answer do you give to somebody who says, "If God loves us, He would not allow us to suffer such pain"?

I do not believe in this statement and I feel comfortable about sharing my own beliefs about God and about the meaning of suffering with my patients without attempting to impose my own values, my own philosophy and religious beliefs onto them.

You said we should build on the specific hopes of the dying. How integrative is this if the basis of those hopes appears to be unrealistic?

When a terminally ill patient, who has very little chance to live more than a few months, expresses the hope of living many more years this is a very, very realistic expression of his present feelings. I have no trouble saying to the patient, "Wouldn't that be great?" This is a way of expressing my understanding of his wishes and simultaneously saying that it is perhaps a dream that cannot be fulfilled. We always share the hopes of our dying patients if we genuinely feel this way. If a young mother who is dying says, "I hope this research laboratory works hard so I get one of their miracle drugs and I will get cured," I know that the chances for this to become a reality are extremely slim, but I have no trouble sharing her hopes with her because I, too, would like her to respond to a new drug and be able to get home to her children.

Would you comment on the dimensions of hope from a patient's point of view which may be different from the hope as perceived by the health team.

There are two basic types of hope and they should be differentiated. At the beginning of a terminal illness, hope is almost exclusively associated with cure, treatment, and prolongation of life. This is true for the patient, the family, and the staff. When these three are no longer probable—and I'm not saying "possible" because there are always exceptions—then the hope of the terminally ill patient changes to something that is no longer associated with cure, treatment, or prolongation of life. His hopes then are more short term or have something to do with life after death or the people he is leaving behind. For example, a young mother who was dying changed her hope shortly before her death with the statement, "I hope my children can make it." Another woman, who was religious, said to me, "I hope God will accept me in His garden." It is imperative that we listen to the patient and strengthen his hopes and do not project our own, otherwise we cannot really help our patients.

What happens when a patient never apparently experiences any stage of anger, never asks why? Would faith be a reason for this?

Yes, a patient with great faith may not question why this is happening to him. If the patient has reached a genuine stage of acceptance before he is terminally ill, he never goes through the stage of anger.

What do you think of saying to a dying patient, "Maybe this is the Lord's will"?

I don't like this answer. It is often used as "an easy way out" and not very helpful, often only resulting in more anger directed at clergy and God.

Do people who do not have a concept of immortality have a harder time working through the different stages?

Not necessarily. It does not matter whether your religious belief includes a specific belief in immortality. It is more relevant that whatever you are, whatever religious beliefs you have, you are genuine and authentic. We have seen very few people who do not believe in some form of immortality. For some, it is the work they have left behind. Others continue to live through their children, while still others believe in a resurrection or in an actual life after death.

Have you dealt with an atheist and how did he or she accept death?

We have worked with only four genuine, true atheists and they have died with amazing peace and acceptance, no different from a religious person.

How does one deal with the dying patient who has no religious faith or denies having any? How does one offer comfort and/or meaning?

There are many ways of offering comfort to a dying patient and this should not be dependent on his religious faith. Comfort means your being with him, giving him physical comfort, pain relief, back rubs, moving him around if he is unable to move, holding his hand, listening to his needs. This way you can help patients whether they have faith or no faith. Real love and faith is often conveyed better by action than by words.

Research is a valuable experience yet does not equal the experience itself. How can one in a helping profession really understand?

Nobody knows for sure what truth is. We can only approximate it. I think we can identify with our dying patients and get a glimpse of it which does not mean that we really understand the full meaning of it. It is better to ask questions and to try to find answers than to look away and thus avoid the issue and the dying patient.

What sorts of hopes are expressed by patients in the acceptance stage of dying?

The hopes are usually related to family members who are left behind, the hope that they have left an imprint here on earth, the hope that they have raised their children to be independent enough so that they can stand on their own feet, and the hope that God will accept them in His garden. Many patients associate their final hope with "I hope I can keep my dignity" or "I hope God will relieve this suffering soon." It is important that you strengthen the patient's hope and do not project your own hopes, which will most likely be associated with cure, treatment, or prolongation of life.

On Sunday I was talking to a returned missionary and mentioned to her that I was going to attend a seminar on death and dying. She immediately asked if you were a "Christian" and then went on to elaborate and say the only important thing was to know if the patient was "ready" and knew the "Lord." I knew what she believes but I could only conjure a mental picture of someone running into each patient's room asking if they were "ready to die." How do you break through to these deeply religious people to make them see that there are more facets to dying than the one mentioned above?

I do not regard these people as truly religious, because if they were really such good Christians, they would accept every human being as "thy neighbor" and not judge them as good or bad depending on whether they were Christians or non-Christians.

In your experience, do intensely religious people accept death more easily than most others?

Yes, if they are authentic and have internalized their faith.

Do you believe that a deep faith in God—Christian or otherwise—is helpful in facing death? Is it detrimental to some people when that faith replaces medical help?

I think you are talking about Christian Scientists. We have seen many cases where patients believed that faith alone could make them physically well and they sought medical help too late. For those people, this kind of faith has been detrimental. I do believe that medicine and faith have to work together, but one must not exclude the other.

In your work with the dying patient, have you noticed a difference between the Christian dying patient and the non-Christian as to how they accept death?

We have worked with many more Christian patients than non-Christians. The significant variable is not *what* you believe, but *how* truly and genuinely you believe. People who have believed in reincarnation, or people from Eastern cultures and religions have often accepted death with unbelievable peace and equanimity even at a young age; whereby many of our Christian patients have had difficulties in their acceptance of death. Only the few true genuine religious people have accepted death with great peace and equanimity; but in our counseling we have seen very few of these people, because we are usually called for consultations to those patients who are troubled. I would say that about 95 percent of our patients that we have studied have been a little bit religious, but not genuine and authentic. They then have the additional concern about punishment after death, regrets and guilt about missed opportunities.

In your experience, how do you see a deep, abiding relationship with God as making death meaningful and "easier"—excuse the word—to bear?

Truly religious people with a deep abiding relationship with God have found it much easier to face death with equanimity. We do not often see them because they aren't troubled, so they don't need our help.

Will a person with a firm belief in his religion (for example, a Catholic belief in a better life in heaven) go through these same stages of dying?

Yes, religious people also go through the same stages of dying, but quicker and with less turmoil.

In what way do you feel that prayers assist patients and their families to face death?

I believe in the help of prayer, if a patient or a family asks for it. If you are not sure don't simply go in and visit the dying patient and pray with him. Ask him first if he wants a prayer. If he says yes, then go ahead and pray but don't use a prayer book. Listen to your own heart and soul and talk spontaneously rather than reading out of a prepared text. Such spontaneous, honest prayer offered by a caring human being can often help more than many tranquilizers.

13

Personal Questions

Many students of mine have asked how any one person can spend so much time in caring for "hopeless patients," what gives us the strength or conviction to do this kind of "sad work" over a long period of time. A few answers to some of these questions may help you to understand where our resources come from and how we cope with the problem of overinvolvement to the detriment of our own well-being.

It has to be emphasized that I also care for non-terminally ill patients, that I have a house, a family, a garden to take care of. I do not believe that anyone should work exclusively with dying patients five days a week, or nine hours a day. This work is extremely exhausting and emotionally draining. Each of us has to find his own way of "recharging the battery" before we are too drained and unable to give of ourselves.

How do you keep your own emotional balance and not feel overwhelmed or depressed working so totally in this field of dying? I find this a real question for me

and would appreciate your speaking on this point,
i.e., how to feel with, but not overidentify or get
overwhelmed.

I find working with dying patients very gratifying.
Although it is sad many times, I don't find it depress-
ing. It is important to state that I am not doing this
work full time. I also see other, non-terminal patients,
some psychiatric, and some not. I see patients who are
getting well again and patients who have a chance to
live. When you work with the families of leukemic
children you find that many of these children go into
remission, they are able to start nursery school, they
are able to start first grade. You experience the happi-
ness of children who are able to graduate from high
school when they never expected to reach this goal,
and you see young girls who are able to fall in love
and live every day at its fullest. You share not only
the sad low points with the families of these dying
children, but you are also able to share the highlights
with the families. When you work with dying patients,
you develop a meaningful relationship with the families of these patients. Many of the widows and wid-
owers will contact me months and years after the
death of a patient, and tell me about a planned wed-
ding or a confirmation of a child. In this way I take
part in every aspect of their living, and not only in the
deaths in their families. The emotional balance naturally also comes from my own happy family, from
having an understanding husband and two healthy
children, from having a home and a garden where I
can work, from vacations which I take regularly, and
from climbing in the mountains of Switzerland and
Alaska, where I can forget about my work and my
patients for a couple of weeks every year.

Are your views motivated by religion or a unique philosophy?

I don't think I started this work motivated by religion. When I started to work with dying patients, I was certainly not regarded as a religious person. Working with dying patients over many years has made me much more religious than I have ever been. It has also become a philosophy of life, one that I certainly learned from my terminally ill patients.

What does acceptance of your own death mean to you?

It means to me that I am ready to die whenever the time comes; that I'll try at least to live every day as if it were my last one, and, needless to say, hope for a thousand more days like today.

How many patients were you with at the actual moment of death; what did you say or do?

I have not been with many patients at the actual moment of death. My work generally takes place before death occurs. I see that my patients are taken care of in every way that we can take care of human beings. When I had the privilege of being with them at the actual moment of death, I don't think I ever said a word. You just sit with them and hold their hand, or if there are family members present you very often have to hold their hands harder than the dying patient's hand.

In all your research on death, what is your personal belief of what happens after death?

Before I started working with dying patients, I did not believe in a life after death. I now do believe in a life after death, beyond a shadow of a doubt.

How do you manage your life so that you can see people at the right time and still have time for your family?

You can only do this if the number of patients you have is not excessive. If I have more than about ten terminally ill patients at one time who are close to dying, then I reach a point where I cannot be with them when they need me. This is why you have to have a good intradisciplinary team of people who are available when the patient needs you. I have to go home sometimes. I try to cook dinner for my family; I often have to go to school or take my girl to the Girl Scouts or my son for another event at school. My family needs me and their needs have to come first. But I do have nurses, ministers, social workers, and physicians who can be available when I am physically not available to my patients. I try to be reachable day and night. My patients have my home telephone number and the demand on my family in regard to telephone calls is sometimes excessive, but they have learned to accept this as part of life and as perhaps their contribution to my work.

How do you personally deal with the repeated loss of so many patients?

I have so many good and wonderful and sometimes unique experiences with my dying patients. We go together through the stages and reach the stage of acceptance together. When the patient dies, I often feel good about it because he is relieved of his suffering and is at peace. Thus I feel I have done the best I could while he was alive. I then have to be able to wean off, to separate myself from this relationship and make my energy available to another patient. I think the art is not how not to get involved, but how to get deeply involved and be able to "switch gears again." I feel sad when they die, but not depressed.

Would you please tell us how you feel about your own death; what does your own death mean to you?

Peace!

How long did it take for the stage of acceptance and living each day as it comes to become a part of your own personal attitude and that of your family?

I think this takes years. I grew up in Switzerland, which is a much less death-denying society so that I was perhaps a little bit ahead. Working with dying patients gradually eliminates your own fear of death, and without your conscious awareness you become much more like your dying patients in their last stage of acceptance. Exactly when this happened is very hard to evaluate, but I'm sure it took me years of working with dying patients.

If you feel like crying when you are with a dying patient, do you cry with them, or how do you respond?

I have had many tears with many of my dying patients and I'm not ashamed of them, nor do I feel that this is "not professional."

How has this work with dying people affected you?

It has made my life much more meaningful and much richer.

How do you, if you do, protect yourself emotionally in your relationships with terminally ill patients?

I dare to get emotionally involved with them. This saves me the trouble of using half of my energy to cover up my feelings.

With all your background, can you say that you are willing to accept your own death?

Yes.

How do you emotionally cope with the loss of patients you have grown close to?

You say goodbye to them knowing that this is the last goodbye, as you learn to say goodbye to people at the railroad station or an airport when you know that they are going far away and you don't know for how long or if you will ever see them again.

When I first found out about my terminal illness I realized that my future had been taken away from me. Would you have similar feelings?

I am sure that most of my patients who realized for the first time that they had a terminal illness had a feeling of agony and anguish and viewed it as a deprivation of their future. This is a very normal reaction and usually does not last long. Then they begin to concentrate on the now and the here and begin to live more fully, with more awareness, more depth, and more intensity every day because they do not have much of a future. A few years ago I would have reacted the same way.

Deep down do you believe that you are immortal?

I believe that our bodies die but the spirit or soul is immortal.

How is your program funded? Would you always recommend that death and dying services be without charge to the patient?

My programs are not funded. I have never charged a terminally ill patient nor his family, regardless of the financial situation. I am giving workshops and lectures throughout the United States, Canada, and Europe and get an honorarium for my lectures. This enables me to see all my patients free of charge. I have never received any grants or any monies from anywhere else. I believe that working with terminally ill patients is a service similar to ones that the clergy perform. I cannot see charging a fee to a dying patient. Not only because terminal and prolonged illness is extremely expensive in the United States, but because this is a humanitarian service which should not be paid for the money. I think those of us who do this work part time have to find other means of support for ourselves and our families. Though I would not like my husband to subsidize my work, there is a distinct advantage in being a woman who does not have to support a family.

How would you tell your children that you had a fatal illness and will probably die soon?

I would sit with each one individually and would
tell them that I am seriously ill and then listen to their
questions and answer all of them openly, frankly, and
honestly. Since we are not always "privileged" to
have a fatal illness, and thus time to prepare our family, we should raise our children to be prepared for a
death in the family at any time. We should live each
day as if it were the last one and enjoy every moment
we have together. Along with the appreciation of having
fully lived, memories are the only real gifts we can
leave our children.

Index